Abilene's War
With Whiskey

and Other Hometown Commotions

Abilene's War With Whiskey

and Other Hometown Commotions

Jay Moore

The cover photo is the personalized license plate on Dallas
Perkins's 1977 Cadillac.
(Courtesy of the *Abilene Reporter-News*)

Design by Lauren Monsey,
Monsey Creative LLC

Cover design by London Moore

ISBN: 979-8-9873351-8-5

Published by Texas Star Trading Company
174 Cypress Street, Abilene, Texas
www.TexasStarTrading.com
(325) 672-9696

Printed in the USA

Contents

Things fall apart; the center cannot hold.

William Butler Yeats

Preface

Commotions seem to crop up with little warning and then, before you know it, they have sprouted into headline news. They might first spark to life when a well-meaning advocate speaks up to challenge the status quo, or a trailblazer calls a press conference to announce things are about to go a different direction, or some injured citizen gets a burr under his saddle and instructs the attorneys to take legal action. However it starts, once a few apples get knocked off the proverbial apple cart, human nature kicks in and in no time at all opinions are zinging back and forth across the public square. And, voila!, you've got the necessary ingredients for a full-blown hullabaloo.

Such dust-ups might involve a vast swath of the citizenry with just about everyone falling in with one side or the other. Or there might be a small, highly-convicted group strongly set on regulating activities affecting the whole, such as which movies we can see or even which day those movies can be shown (see "Not Tonight Henry!" and "Sunday Movies at the Paramount").

Then there are lesser squabbles affecting smaller groups; maybe just two people lock horns, such as when the mayor conks a city commissioner in the head with a trash can ("Mayor York and Commissioner Johnson") or a group of college boys feel the sting of disrespect ("The Ambushing of Texas Tech"). Others wage their battles while the rest of us occupy a ringside seat.

Such spats are drawn along a variety of battle lines. But, oftentimes — at least in Abilene — that line is deeply rooted in religion. And, from the safety of our respective moral trenches, we lob our dogma at the other side, pushing back against their viewpoint: pro-this v. anti-that. (I find that very few people ever stake out a position in the high middle ground. Probably too lonely there.)

It is a sure bet that the longest, most contentious, and most divisive commotion to crop up in the history of Abilene was whether or not our town would be wet or dry; should we openly sell alcohol or not? And religion certainly was a factor in that protracted fight. For many, it was a personal struggle, as their public stance did not sync up with their private behavior. Don't worry, I didn't name names or rat out any Baptists disguising their cocktail in a coffee mug. The story of Abilene's drawn-out "War With Whiskey" is the first part of this book.

And, just for the record, my personal habit is to not drink, a decision based less on principled piety and more on simply being cheap, plus a nagging sense that if I ever got going, I might have a hard time putting on the brakes. I am perfectly content with your choice and the principled stance pushing you to lean whichever way you happen to lean. And, in Abilene, most everyone leans one way or the other.

Following that tale, I have attempted a retelling of several lesser commotions that have flared up along the way and added a bit of momentary drama to the local scene.

Of course, no group of people are immune; commotions crop up in every place — even in a town full of very nice folks, like Abilene.

PART ONE:
Abilene's War With Whiskey

Introduction

When the Sunday edition of the *Abilene Reporter-News* landed on front lawns all across Abilene on June 4, 1978, tucked inside were ads, articles and letters regarding the liquor election less than two weeks away. Once again, the electorate was preparing to go to the polls and once more render a verdict on the legal sale of alcohol in Abilene; or to be more accurate, sales in Precinct 1 of Taylor County, which contains nearly all of Abilene.

In those pre-social media days, advocates on both sides expressed their thoughts using the most effective method available, the newspaper. There were no emojis or memes, just words, yet one had no trouble discerning the emotions and the passion. You could feel that some convictions were being shouted, others were attempts to cajole. And you knew others were written with at least a hint of exasperation. Still, it is doubtful that any voters were swayed by the harangues of those on the other side. Principles aren't changed that easily.

Only two years earlier an identical referendum had been

placed before Abilene voters, and now the whole disruptive
melodrama was playing out once again. In the hard-fought
1976 vote, more than 24,000 people — nearly 60 percent of
eligible voters — showed up to vote their beliefs. (A typical
Abilene voter turnout for local elections is less than 20
percent, often considerably less.)

Now, two years later, with the rancorous odor of 1976
still lingering in the air, the options were the same as before:
maintain the status quo by not allowing the sale of booze in
Abilene or, make a switch, ending seven decades of drought,
and go wet, putting beer, wine and John Barleycorn out in full
view in restaurants, bars, grocery stores, and undisguisedly
into the lives of the innocents living in Precinct 1. And many
succumbed to the need to voice their mind about the matter.

Printed at the top of Page 5 in that June 1978 Sunday
edition was a letter to the editor. It was written in response to
a letter which appeared a week earlier. The earlier letter was
from Mr. Larry Legg, who chimed in on the upcoming wet /
dry vote from the confines of his prison cell at the Ellis Unit
in Huntsville where he was serving a life sentence. (He was
convicted of a 1976 Abilene burglary and sentenced to ten
years but, following an escape from the Taylor County jail in
1977, he was deemed "habitual" and given a life sentence.)
Despite his circumstances, he maintained a healthy interest
in hometown debates.

In his letter, Legg urged Abilene voters to approve alcohol
sales. He noted, "I, myself, have nothing against religion and
everyone should have a taste of it. This upcoming liquor

election has nothing to do with religion." He concluded with, "Vote 'Yes' in the liquor election and remember Jesus turned the water into wine." Now, a week later, Abilenians brought the paper in from their lawn, sat down with their coffee, and at the top of Page 5 read a letter in response to Mr. Legg's throwaway line about Jesus turning water to wine.

The seven-paragraph letter was signed, "Sincerely, The Young People of Trinity Baptist Church," and listed the names of thirty-five Abilene teens. Assuming their youth minister did not write the letter and urge them to put their names to it, the students impressed — using words such as "preclude," "insinuation," and "interchangeably." They pointed out that the Greek word for wine was "oinos," adding that it was "a general term used interchangeably to refer to any number of derivatives from the grape, i.e. juice, vinegar, syrup or fermented juice." They went on to explain the laws of fermentation and the effect of temperature on grape juice and how it would quickly turn to vinegar since, in Jesus' time, there was no way to cool it except in caves and "not everyone had a cave." Remarkably, the group was familiar with the writings of Plato, Pliny, Homer and Cicero and further noted that the ancients recorded that in biblical times the drink of choice was not wine but rather a honey-like syrup.

In their final paragraph, the youth group issued a collective indictment of Mr. Legg's intellect, exclaiming that his statement about Jesus turning water into wine was "based on ignorance." They ended their broadside by lobbing an insult: "Furthermore, it is our opinion that Mr. Legg's taste for liquor receives far more attention than his taste for religion." Ouch! They punctuated the whole thing with, "Proverbs 20:1," but leaving it up to Legg and other readers to look up their coup de grace: "Wine is a mocker, strong drink is raging: and whosoever is deceived thereby is not wise." Wise or not, at least Mr. Legg cast no aspersions.

Ironically, neither inmate Legg nor many of the Trinity Baptist youth would be eligible to vote on the matter. He was a convicted felon and indefinitely absent from the county; many of the church kids were too young. Regardless, all felt the need to be heard.

Quoting scripture was an oft-used and favored weapon in the arsenal of both Wets and Drys, including Christians who were opposed to hypocrisy more than they were to alcohol sales. On the same page as the youth group letter was one from Abilene resident Robert Williams urging his fellow Christians to not overlook the words of Timothy in his first New Testament letter, Chapter 5, Verse 23: "No longer drink water exclusively, but use a little wine for the sake of your stomach and your frequent ailments." Indeed, Abilene suffered from a frequent ailment.

For the first twenty-two years of the city's history, anti-prohibitionists — i.e., Wets — had things their way. That was followed by a marathon stretch of seventy-five years where the teetotalers — Drys — held sway. The pendulum has since swung back the other way, and as of 2024, the Friendly Frontier has been wet for more than four and a half decades.

Since the city's earliest days, Abilene has wrestled with the alcohol question, not because the residents are uncertain, indecisive or irresolute. Quite the opposite. The city has struggled because we are divided largely in two equal groups, each one very certain, very decisive, and with heels-dug-in resolve. For those opposed to the legal sale of alcohol in Abilene, their will was heavily pinned on the word "openly." They were well aware that during the decades in which Abilene was legally dry, it was not a big chore to get one's hands and lips on the stuff, either illegally within the city limits or quite legally just a few miles north or south of town. But there was an acceptable quid pro quo: with a small effort drinkers could find their intoxicants, while the anti-alcohol crowd could bask in the moral pride felt from living in a "dry" city. Liquor was not out in the open in Abilene!

In addition to their moral arguments, the Drys preached that open sale of alcohol would produce a litany of attendant social issues if intoxicants were allowed out into the light of day. They cited statistics from other cities that bore out their belief that Old Demon Rum had offspring! After all, do we want to be Bedford Falls or Pottersville?

For the Wets, the issue was less straightforward. For some, it was a matter of Texas spirit — "No one's going to tell me what I can or can't do." For others, the inconvenience of long drives to liquor stores or having to pay private club fees to drink within the city was unnecessary and a bit irritating. For still others, the matter was one of economics; they pointed out that legal sales of alcohol would benefit county and city tax coffers, creating lower taxes. Wets also cited their own statistics, ones that did not bear out the ancillary problems that the Drys predicted as inevitable; in other cities where alcohol sales were legalized, murder rates, public intoxication, and DWI arrests had not suddenly soared, skid rows had not sprung up.

———

The debate over whether alcohol should be openly sold in Abilene has long stirred deep passions on both sides. At times, the debate has been quite civil, even mature, while at other times, the tenor leaned mean, vindictive, and impolite; we were not on our best behavior, and a few embarrassed themselves with immature antics. Indeed, it has been a long, slow and, at times, strange roller-coaster ride.

*Deputy Marshal Walter Collins and Zeno Hemphill
were buried this evening, and a large concourse of people
followed each to the cemetery.*

Galveston Daily News
reporting on "The Abilene Tragedy," January 9, 1883

1881 - 1903: Wet

More than once, temperance movements have swept across America. In the 1830s and '40s, prompted in part by Protestant churches that first urged moderation, then changed tactics and appealed for resistance to temptation, there was a rising call for government, at all levels, to wholesale ban the stuff. A second temperance wave took place in the 1880s with many state legislatures voting on the matter and, in some states, including Texas, submitting the prohibition question to their citizens in the form of state constitutional amendments. Texans were set to vote on such an amendment in the summer of 1887. By then, young Abilene was still trying to figure out who we were, having been a town for only six years.

In the pages of *The Taylor County News*, readers were urged to vote for the state prohibition amendment and offered up "Thirty Reasons for the Prohibition of the Traffic in Intoxicating Liquors." Among the reasons listed for outlawing liquors:

1. They deprive men of their reason for the time being.

7. They cause many thousands of murders.

11. They cause the majority of cases of insanity.

17. Because moderate drinkers want the temptation removed.

18. Because drunkards want the temptation removed.

19. Because sober people want the temptation removed.

28. It is contrary to the Bible.

Texans went to the polls to decide if the state constitution would be amended to read: "The manufacture, sale, and exchange of intoxicating liquors, except for medical, mechanical, sacramental, and scientific purposes, is hereby prohibited in the State of Texas."

Statewide the proposal went down in lopsided defeat by a vote of 220,627 to 129,270. However, Abilene and Taylor County voters bucked the majority. All seven voting locations in the county returned a majority in favor of prohibition. In Abilene prohibition was favored 311 to 188.

1880s

As the Texas and Pacific Railway laid down its rails, cutting a swath across northern Taylor County in February 1881, a reporter from the *Shreveport Times* wrote, "Abilene is the 'loud locality' now. There are over 1,000 people there occupying tents and boarding cars. There are several saloons opened." And that was a month before Abilene was born.

Saloons sprang up early in the life of Abilene, as did churches. Two weeks prior to the town lot auction, the Presbyterians gained an early foothold when a group of nine believers met on Sunday morning, February 27, at Pine and North 1st to establish First Presbyterian Church.

Fourteen days later, Abilene formally came to be when auctioneer James Hosack mounted a makeshift stage composed of stacked railroad ties and gavelled the crowd of several hundred to order on a cold Tuesday morning. The group was made up of land speculators, stout-hearted easterners willing to take a chance on a new community, and a sizable presence of Buffalo Gappers who traveled twelve miles north, curious about the upstart town in the northeast corner of Taylor County. The auction to create the town of Abilene spanned two days with more than 300 lots sold on March 15 and 16.

Soon, train cars from Weatherford, stacked with lumber, began to arrive and the charter Abilenians were busy, hammering together homes, businesses and churches. And saloons.

Quick on the heels of the auction, the Baptists, Methodists, Christians and Episcopalians got going, ready to quench the local spiritual thirst. But another type of thirst could be just as readily quenched. In those early years, saloons often outnumbered churches, and it was a toss-up as to which had a greater weekly attendance. You could fill your soul as easily as you could wet your whistle. Prominently situated at North 1st and Pine, catty-corner to the spot where the Presbyterians organized, stood the Cattle Exchange saloon.

Two doors down from the Cattle Exchange was the White Elephant Saloon. There was Harrington's on Pine, and right next door to it was a two-story building with the Maverick Saloon. On the first floor they were serving up "Old Crow" while attorneys were serving up legal advice one flight up. Mel Thompson's saloon was at South 1st at Oak. A block south on Oak was the Little Red Saloon. There was the National, where the top whiskey was "Old Forester." You could drink at the Gilt Edge, the T&P Saloon, or the Arcade, known for a wide selection of wines selected by owner W.A. Gray. Gus Ackerman, a Belgian immigrant, was pouring "Oscar Pepper" at the Delmonico, while a Mr. Hamblin ran the First & Last Chance Saloon on Pine. The beer parlors and their gambling games meant you could lose your sobriety as well as your money. You could also get shot.

In 1885 county animal inspector W.T. Gilstrap and a guy named Johnson from Colorado City got into a dispute over a game of cards in Harrington's Saloon, culminating in two shots that turned Gilstrap's wife into a widow. On a warm August morning that same year, George Wilson, the bartender at Mel Thompson's saloon, had a heated exchange with Jim Bird before Wilson brandished a lemon squeezer and ran Bird off. A half hour later Bird returned, pointing his gun at Wilson who ducked behind the bar. As Bird turned to leave, Wilson opted for a more deadly weapon this time and shot Bird as he was crossing Oak Street. He died on the spot.

Rivers Bolank was drinking in W.A. Gray's Arcade Saloon in 1890 when he pulled a knife on bartender Bob Burch. In turn, Burch pulled out a gun and fired one shot at Bolank, who staggered across the tracks to the White Elephant and died next to the bar there.

For the first two years, Abilene was fairly well untamed. But in January 1883 the citizens voted to incorporate as a town, establishing a governmental structure and electing a mayor, aldermen and a city marshal. One of the first orders of business was to pass an ordinance regulating city life and put a halt to gambling inside the city limits. Gambling was readily available in the saloons, with options ranging from cards to billiards to pigeonhole – a table game where you tried to roll small balls into openings at the far end. An ordinance banning all such activity was quickly put into effect. Enforcing the ban led to the city's deadliest shootout.

In 1884 Zeno Hemphill and the Collins brothers pulled out their weapons inside the Cattle Exchange, ending each of their lives. Zeno Hemphill was well known to the city marshal as he had a deserved reputation for being hot-headed. He had shot and killed Rose Breeding in 1883 but walked free following a hung jury. Months later, he was working at the Cattle Exchange when Walter and Frank Collins came in to talk to Hemphill about his flagrant violation of the recently enacted city gambling ordinance. Walter was a deputy marshal and brother Frank was an alderman on the city council.

Inside the saloon, the conversation quickly became heated and Frank Collins drew his pistol to gain the upper hand. In response, Hemphill struck Collins in the head with a fist. Walter rushed between his brother and Hemphill to put a stop to the argument, but Hemphill drew his pistol, shooting Walter in the chest. Suddenly gunfire erupted all around. When the smoke cleared, all three were lying on the floor. Hemphill, shot seven times, died within seconds. Walter lingered for half an hour. Frank suffered four gunshots, dying two months later from his wounds. (Ironically, Zeno Hemphill and the Collins brothers are buried only a few yards apart at the city cemetery. Zeno disliked having the sun in his eyes, so his brother Marcus insisted that Zeno's casket be oriented at a slant, with his brother's head to the northwest so the eastern sun would not bother him.) A historical marker at North 1st and Pine notes the events of that deadly day, one that served to punctuate Abilene's early wet years.

Despite the violence and the anti-gambling ordinance, saloons and the selling of alcohol remained legal in Abilene. Since the defeat of the statewide prohibition amendment in 1887, the only recourse to close local saloons was for the aldermen to pass such an ordinance. Then, in 1891, when Abilene was ten years old, a new option arose.

1891

Texans went to the polls in August 1891 to decide on five

proposed amendments to the state constitution. (As of 2024, the Texas constitution is among the longest of any state and has been amended more than 500 times.) Three days after the vote, the *Abilene Reporter* noted the local response. "The election passed off quietly here on Tuesday. A very light vote was polled. Very little interest was shown in the election." One of the amendments approved statewide provided "for voters of any county, precinct, town or city, by a majority vote, from time to time, may determine whether the sale of intoxicating liquors shall be prohibited." It is a course of action known as "local option." (Today, seventeen states bar any of their counties from being dry; in other words, the option is not local.)

With passage of the amendment, Taylor County, like all Texas counties, was granted the option of deciding if, from time to time, they wanted to be wet or dry. The same option applied to any smaller political subdivision within the county. The ever-changing citizenry of Taylor County has made good use of that constitutional provision, from time to time. The first time was in 1894.

1894

A petition with more than 400 signatures was submitted to the county commissioners in February 1894 requesting a countywide local option election. Two weeks later a group of Abilene ministers assembled at the county courthouse to organize a strategy for passing the proposed ban on alcohol and shuttering local saloons. The *Abilene Reporter* came out against the proposition, fearing that replacing legal saloons with unregulated bootleggers willing to sell whiskey to "your minor sons who could not get it in a public saloon," was a risk too great to take. The local option vote took place on March 10. Favoring an end to alcohol were 496 voters, while 610 were opposed. By 114 votes, Taylor County remained wet. Eight years later a second local option vote was put before county voters.

1902

The pastors of First Baptist Church and First Methodist Church circulated petitions for a local option election aiming to outlaw booze and put a halt to saloons and the troubles they seemed to breed. Following a long and contentious run-up, the local option election to decide if Taylor County would be wet or dry arrived on June 7, 1902. This time, things went a different way. By a vote of 1,196 to 966 — a 230-person majority — Taylor County prohibitionists managed to dry things up, banishing alcohol and forcing Abilene saloons to close. Bar owners were given ten months to get things in order and find another line of work.

Gus Ackerman shuttered Delmonico's Saloon sooner than required after finding employment as bookkeeper for Western Compress. Saloonkeeper Ike Brown filed suit against the leader of the prohibition movement, claiming that the instigator had "maliciously aroused and stirred up the people of Taylor County," thus bringing damage to Brown's business in the range of $10,000.

On the same day that Taylor County voted dry, a local option election was held next door in Callahan County. They went the other way, voting wet. At least two Abilene saloon owners pulled up stakes and moved their businesses to Baird.

It would be difficult to find in all the country a city
whose inhabitants are so uniformly of a high moral type.
Taylor County voted out saloons by an overwhelming majority
and it is the pride of her people that the local option law
is strictly enforced.

The Western Evangel, 1907

1903 - 1959: Dry

1903

The ban on selling alcohol in Taylor County took effect at the stroke of midnight on April 10, 1903. Minutes before, Abilene saloon keepers poured their last legal drinks, capped the bottles, turned out the lights and shut their doors. It would be seventy-five years before the next drink was legally poured in a public bar in Abilene.

The lack of saloons was a point of pride as well as a selling point for the local colleges. The 1904 Simmons College (now Hardin-Simmons University) catalog advised prospective students that "Abilene has no saloons and is free from many of the temptations found in larger cities, yet it affords nearly all their social and educational advantages." The 1906 catalog for Abilene Christian noted, "Abilene is a quiet, clean, moral little city of about ten thousand inhabitants. There are no saloons and grog shops here, and low, vicious characters are not tolerated. Nearly all the churches are represented and each student is expected to attend the services of one of them."

Despite the dry conditions, one could still find a drink in Abilene. One early Abilene resident told of a funeral operator who kept a keg of what he called "embalming fluid" in the back of his business. In the evening, men would often drop by "to view the body" and get a swig of that embalming fluid.

1911

Once again, in 1911, the Texas legislature referred a constitutional amendment promoting temperance to the voters. A "yes" vote indicated you supported the enactment of a statewide prohibition on the manufacture and sale of alcoholic beverages.

Abilene's fairer sex urged "yes" votes and made their thoughts known in a newspaper ad: "WE, THE WOMEN OF ABILENE, in the fear of God and in the name of all that is holy, just and true, do most earnestly petition your friends, brothers, fathers and husbands to remember mother, wife, home and God and vote for prohibition on the 22nd day of July, 1911. If because of past pledge or otherwise, you cannot consistently vote for us, please refrain from voting at all."

Taylor Countians did not disappoint the ladies. By more than two to one, the county voted in favor of the state being dry.

Early statewide returns were favorable to the Drys, or the "yes" crowd. Across page one of the Sunday morning *Abilene Reporter* the headline read, "TEXAS VOTES DRY BY LIGHT MAJORITY." But, in fact, not all the votes had been counted and, once they were, the results swung the other way. Out of the nearly 470,000 votes cast, the difference was 6,300. Abilene ladies were disappointed. The state of Texas would not be constitutionally dry. Of course, nothing changed for Abilene.

1918 - 1919

Congress sent the Eighteenth Amendment to the states for ratification in December 1917. Texas was an early supporter, being the eighth state to approve the constitutional change when the Texas legislature ratified it on March 4, 1918.

When Nebraska became the thirty-sixth state to ratify the amendment (thus fulfilling the requisite approval of three-fourths of the forty-eight states) on January 16, 1919, Prohibition became the law of the land. The rest of America officially followed Abilene's lead.

Just for good measure, in 1919 Texas voters went ahead and added a statewide prohibition amendment to the Texas Constitution. Of course, Abilene and Taylor County voters gave it wide approval.

The Eighteenth Amendment banned the manufacture, sale, and transportation of alcoholic beverages. Ten months later, Congress enacted the Volstead Prohibition Enforcement Act creating a mechanism for enforcing prohibition. Both laws took effect on January 16, 1920. Again, the constitutional amendment had no effect in Abilene since the citizens were already on board with the idea. But Prohibition turned out to be a bad idea.

1933

Mounting the bandstand located on the Federal Lawn behind the post office, McMurry College president James Hunt addressed a crowd of 2,000, urging voters to oppose ratification of the Twenty-First Amendment which would reverse the Eighteenth and make alcohol legal once again in America. President James Cox of Abilene Christian College reiterated Hunt's position, as did a host of preachers. The statewide vote was scheduled for the next day, August 26.

Texans voted overwhelmingly to do away with the Eighteenth Amendment. Once more, Taylor County voters felt otherwise. The Twenty-First Amendment was voted down in Taylor County (2,522 to 1,653) with only five of the thirty ballot boxes voting to repeal.

It was widely expected that other states would vote just as Texas, so, while waiting for enough states to act and undo Prohibition nationwide, President Franklin Roosevelt amended the Volstead Act to allow people to have a beer or two while waiting on ratification. In celebration, Budweiser sent its Clydesdales to the White House to deliver a case of beer.

The Great Experiment turned out to be the Great Failed Experiment. The fourteen years of Prohibition (from January 1920 to December 1933) proved that legislating morality was an unenforceable decree. It also proved that criminals could organize themselves in ways unknown up until that time. The Twenty-First amendment took effect on December 5, 1933 when Utah became the thirty-sixth state to ratify.

Following national repeal of Prohibition, Texans went to the polls again in 1935 to repeal the statewide prohibition law. It passed with 54 percent in favor. In keeping with our contrarian ways, it did not pass in Taylor County, where twice as many voted against repealing Texas prohibition. Texas counties returned to the same wet or dry status which they held before 1919, so Taylor county and Abilene remained bone dry.

With alcohol sales once again legal in most of the state, the legislature created the Texas Liquor Control Board in order to "promote temperance, protect the public interest, encourage observance of the Liquor Control Act, collect taxes and discourage socially undesirable activities such as bootlegging, underage drinking and organized crime." The Board regulated every phase of the liquor business. (In 1970, the Liquor Control Board was renamed the Texas Alcoholic Beverage Commission.)

1934

Following the 1933 repeal of Prohibition, a petition signed by more than 700 Abilene beer proponents requested that County Judge John Camp call a local option election to legalize the sale of beer within the city limits. The local option vote was set for June 30, 1934. On the eve of the election, the anti-beer crowd held a rally on the Federal Lawn and, once again, the group heard from ministers and the three college presidents, each predicting a degradation of Abilene's social and moral fiber if such sales were legalized.

In the second highest turnout for an Abilene election up until that time, 2,801 votes were cast during the Saturday election. After the polls closed, the three telephones at the *Reporter-News* began ringing non-stop as anxious Abilenians called to learn the results. The operators did not bother with "hello," but instead simply repeated over and over, "Still dry by thirty-five votes." Upon hearing the results, one relieved female caller responded, "Thank the Lord for that!" Only to be followed by an "Oh hell!" from a male caller. The slim margin startled some local prohibitionists and emboldened those hoping to make the town wet. They would try again four years later.

1938

A group known as the Business Men's and Taxpayers Association pushed for a local option election to once again make a decision about the sale of beer in the county. The election was held on May 14, 1938, and the turnout was huge. The voting public made an emphatic statement. The banner *Reporter-News* headline read, "Drys Bury Beer Demand Under Ballot Avalanche." Those favoring the legalization of beer totaled 1,971. Those opposed, 4,984. Most notably of all, nearly three-fourths of the county's voting strength turned out. Not a single box polled a wet majority. In Abilene, even the traditionally wet boxes overwhelmingly went dry.

Reverend J.H. Hamblen, pastor of First Methodist and the leader of the effort to remain dry, said, "I want to express the profound gratitude of my heart and thanks to all who so nobly fought for the great dry victory in our city and county. I trust there will be no rankle in the bosom of anyone in this fight but that we may all unite now to make Abilene and Taylor county a cleaner and more wholesome place in which to live."

The wide margin of defeat indeed took the fight out of the dry forces. There would not be another local option election in Abilene for thirty-eight years.

1940s and 1950s

Abilene became host to a U.S. Army training camp in 1941. Camp Barkeley was located nine miles southwest of Abilene and at its height was the twelfth largest "city" in Texas with a population variously reported as between 40,000 and 60,000. Virtually all were young men with a thirst.

In order to slake that thirst, Abilene came to a reconciliation:
the town would be dry, but the soldiers would be given a
pass. More specifically, they could get a prescription for
"medicinal alcohol" that they could fill at any drugstore. By
the busloads, soldiers came to town on Friday and Saturday
nights and were deposited at South 1st and Oak where they
could find several doctors, sitting at tables in the offices of
the Chamber of Commerce, ready and willing to write out
a prescription for a pharmaceutical tonic for the low cost
of twenty-five cents. At times the line of soldiers stretched
around the corner.

Soldiers, along with the rest of Abilene, could also visit
local brown bag clubs where you brought your own alcohol
and, for a fee, the club provided a glass with ice and a mixer.

One of the most popular clubs among Camp Barkeley
soldiers was Charley Blank's Nite Club, located on the Old
Potosi Road (South 14th Street). The club was a rambling
two-story rock structure largely built by Charley himself.
(His name was interchangeably spelled "Charley" and
"Charlie.") He first began working on enlarging a former
Texaco gas station in 1932 and, following five years of work,
opened his night club on May 24, 1937, with ads touting
his barbecued chicken, beef, ham that "Got No Bone" and
duck — "He Can't Talk" — along with his signature Italian
spaghetti — "lotsa spaghetti" served "by the dish, pound or
mile."

Perched in front of the club atop a ten-foot high rock
pedestal was a Charley Blanks original — a concrete

sculpture of a horse-bull creature, surrounded by frogs and ridden by a rifle-toting blank-faced cowboy. When asked what the sculpture was meant to be, Charley would smile and say, "Somethin' I a-make, to a-make-a you ask."

Charley's was a brown bag joint. You brought your own bottle, often in a brown paper bag, and then paid a set-up fee covering the ice and a mixer. More than once, Charley's place was raided by county liquor agents who suspected Charley was providing more than just set-ups. During a 1934 raid, constables confiscated 653 bottles of home brew and hauled Charley off to jail. He was given a five-year suspended sentence. Two years later he was arrested again, this time for "operation of a liquor nuisance southeast of the city." The court ordered his club to be padlocked. Charley was found guilty and assessed a $248 fine and sixty days in jail.

The heyday of Charley Blank's Nite Club was during World War II as a boisterous collection of Barkeley soldiers and officers crowded the concrete booths, ate oversized steaks, and enjoyed the antics of Charley as he took to the bandstand pretending to play along on his light-up saxophone and to remind everyone, "Your bizness is your bizness, and my bizness is my bizness, but no monkey bizness."

Brown bag clubs were largely replaced by private clubs beginning in 1961 with the passage of the Private Club Act which created a path for Texans living in a dry town to access a legal drink. It was illegal to "sell" alcohol in a dry area, but the law provided a work-around so you could be

"served" alcohol. For a minimal membership fee you could
join a private club that was anything but private. If you were
not a member, for a nominal fee you could buy a temporary,
but infinitely renewable, membership. And when a visitor
checked into most Abilene hotels, the room rate included a
membership card for the bar. Many private clubs employed
the locker system, allowing members to store their own liquor
in a club locker. In order to have, say, a rum and Coke, you
poured the rum from your own bottle and the club provided
the Coke.

Other clubs operated under the pool system, where the
members' dues bought the alcohol shared by the members;
in reality, you paid a fee and received liquor by the drink.
Private clubs were spread like oases across an arid Abilene.
You could become a member of the Elmwood West Club, the
Golden Key, the Supper Club, Turf Recreation, Touchdown
Club, the Regular Fellow Recreation Club, the Twenty-Four,
the V.F.W. , or the American Legion. At the Sands Hotel you
could join Club Granada, while at the Downtowner Inn you
could gain access to the Victorian Club. The Bagatel was on
Pine Street, the Bandera on Butternut, and the Dragon Room
was on South 7th. Your membership allowed you to perch
on a bar stool inside the The Ranch House, Top Hat Club,
The Su-Su, or the It'll Do Club. To find a drink in dry Abilene
was not hard; you just needed a card to get through the door.

Favored spots of the business crowd included the
Petroleum Club, the Westwood Club and, the Abilene
Club located on the third floor of the Wooten Hotel. The

Abilene Club was organized in 1930 and opened as part of the hotel but closed in 1962, unable to pay its bills. The club was immediately reformed as the Downtown Abilene Club. Among the three incorporators of the resurrected club was Dallas Perkins.

From the time Abilene closed city saloons in 1903, right up until the early 1960s, if you needed a pint or a keg, it was common knowledge who could surreptitiously meet your need. Bootlegging was a brisk business. The district supervisor for the Liquor Control Board estimated that by 1960 there were around 250 bootleggers doing business in and around Abilene, with some making more than $50,000 a year ($500,000 in 2024 buying power). A twelve-ounce bottle of beer cost fifty cents, a quart went for $1. Whiskey was $5 a pint or $8 for a fifth.

For a city where the sale of alcoholic beverages was legally banned, private clubs and bootleggers offered easy leaps over that hurdle — all done on the sly, behind the doors of private clubs and through discreet cash transactions. Those opposed to such activity could easily look the other way. What so many in Abilene objected to, including bootleggers, was to see beer, wine and whiskey out in the open, on store shelves or listed on restaurant menus, all available for legal purchase. Such a blatant acceptance of alcohol ran counter to the morality and religious doctrine of a "church town." If such sin was not held in check, the poison would spread, corrupting the city's youth like rust eating away at one's soul.

In order to maintain the status quo and avoid a full blown collision of wills, Wets and Drys achieved a tacit agreement — if you wanted to drink in Abilene, then there was plenty of opportunity for you to do so, but it needed to be out of sight. An open smashup between Abilene's acolytes of alcohol and the city's devotedly faithful was an impact to be avoided.

However, the impact was coming.

There are two major problems confronting the United States:
The Berlin Wall crisis and the Impact controversy.

The Haskell Free Press, 1961

1960: Impact

1959

The status quo began to unravel just before midnight on Wednesday, March 11, 1959, when three Texas Rangers, accompanied by Taylor County Sheriff J.D. Woodard and Abilene Police Chief Warren Dodson, walked up the stairs to the front entrance of the Abilene Country Club. Woodard brought along a search warrant. The lawmen had solid information that inside the club was property "for the purpose of gaming, gambling, wagering and betting on gaming and gambling boards, tables and other gambling equipment." In fact, it was no secret that Wednesday evening was "Las Vegas Night" at the club.

The five lawmen entered a room just to the right of the main door. Inside were approximately twenty men — and one woman who had just entered looking for her husband. All were gathered boisterously around two craps tables. It took a few seconds for the dice-shooting crowd to become aware of the newcomers. But as the police presence dawned, the mood noticeably changed and all grew quiet. One Texas Ranger closed the door and positioned himself in front of it. The other lawmen began taking names — names which would appear on the front page of the Abilene newspaper the next morning.

After identifying all present and securing the gaming equipment, the five officers returned outside to Texas Ranger Sgt. John Wood's car, only to find that at least one crapshooter had taken out his frustration; two tires on the patrol car were flat.

Eighteen men were charged with a misdemeanor of "remaining in a place where gaming is unlawfully taking place," with each facing a possible fine. The Country Club manager, Ralph Hunter, was busted with an additional charge, "permitting gambling devices on the premises." Among those facing a maximum penalty of $50 were six out-of-towners and two military officers stationed at Dyess Air Force Base. The balance of the offenders consisted of local men whose addresses were along some of Abilene's silk-stocking streets — Sayles Boulevard, River Oaks Road and Elmwood Drive. Charges were dropped against the lone female who had definitely been in the wrong place at the wrong time.

All of the gamblers pleaded guilty, and County Court

Judge Allen Glenn assessed each the maximum fine. The Country Club wrote a check to cover the entire amount.

Among those charged was a thirty-three-year-old Abilenian by the name of Dallas Guinn Perkins. Perkins was born in Stamford but by age five his family — parents, two brothers and one sister — moved to Abilene where his dad was in the wholesale tobacco business. The family attended First Baptist Church, and young Dallas went to Alta Vista Elementary where he played football and regularly posted perfect attendance. He also joined Boy Scout Troop 7. As a student at Abilene High, he was a member of the Boys Glee Club and a Junior Geologist. Following his 1943 graduation, Perkins enrolled in the U.S. Army Air Services and was accepted into the flight school at Santa Ana Army Air Base in California where he excelled in fighter pilot training. Perkins came home to Abilene for a ten-day leave in October 1944. He and his friend Bill Hensley were out for a spin on Hensley's motorcycle when the pair skidded on some gravel along North 1st Street. Perkins was thrown several yards, hitting his head. He was taken to the hospital at Abilene's Camp Barkeley where he was treated for a fractured skull, an injury that brought an end to his flight training but not to his military service. He continued to serve, stationed at Keesler Field in Biloxi, Mississippi.

Following the war, Perkins returned to Abilene and enrolled at McMurry College but soon determined that college was not for him, so he took a job with Plough Sales, Inc., selling its line of medical products including St. Joseph's aspirin and Mexsana Powder. In November 1949 Perkins married a high school classmate, Nancy Cunningham, in a ceremony at the First Baptist Church. Nancy was a science teacher employed by the Abilene school district; her father, Oliver Cunningham, was an Abilene attorney who had served as a state senator from 1929 to 1933. The Perkinses soon welcomed two sons and a daughter.

The sales job regularly took Perkins away from his young family, so he decided in the late 1950s to become his own boss, opening an advertising agency. He set up his office in the Cypress Building and, since the purpose of any advertising is to make an impact on the potential consumer, Perkins called his business Impact Advertising.

———

Perkins stood well over six feet and stayed thin his whole life. He often wore his hair longer than most Abilene men and bore a slight resemblance to actor Fess Parker. There was a distinct twinkle in his eyes and often a sly grin that revealed the gap between his front teeth; he perpetually looked like he knew something he wasn't telling. He was good about looking you in the eyes and others found him engaging, friendly, a good storyteller, and were drawn to his dry sense of humor, intelligence and confident manner. He was a natural salesman and seldom without a cigarette. (Dallas and Nancy Perkins were friends of my parents, and I was often in his company. My description of him is based on my personal observations and interactions. I knew him to be a walking encyclopedia on Abilene history. Fun fact: The actor Lee Horsley is his nephew. The last time I saw Mr. Perkins was around 2015, when I ran into him in the waiting room of our dentist. I asked him about growing up in Abilene and he recalled stories I wish I'd written down. I hated to walk away when I was called back to the dentist chair.)

The events of that March evening in 1959 at the Country Club prompted Dallas Perkins to make a decision that would alter the trajectory of his business, his life, his family's life and, most assuredly, the culture of Abilene. A few days after the bust, Perkins, still annoyed by what he considered a grandstanding raid and maddened by the overt piety of some in Abilene who clamped down on such activities, joined his usual coffee-drinking group at the Hotel Wooten. Among others, the group included writer and bookstore owner A.C. Greene and attorney Dan Sorrells. Perkins groused about being charged in the gambling raid and rhetorically asked, "Can't a guy just enjoy himself without the Texas Rangers getting involved?" One of his fellow coffee-drinkers quipped, "You can't fight city hall." That flippant comment must have lodged in the mind of Dallas Perkins. He turned to Dan Sorrells and, according to A.C. Greene, said, "Let's form a city."

In a 1966 interview, Perkins maintained he had no intention of creating a town and that the whole idea began as a joke. But just months after the Country Club raid, he bought a twenty acre turkey farm north of Abilene — *barely north* — and when friends asked what he planned to do with the acreage, he jokingly replied, "I'm going to build my own town." Turns out, he was dead serious. And, just like his advertising company, he named it Impact. He could not have chosen a more fitting name.

Few names, if any, more frequently appeared in the Abilene newspaper from 1960 to 1963 than "Dallas Perkins" or "Impact," as he set out to achieve his idea. The path he traveled in order to forge the tiny municipality of Impact, Texas, was strewn with troubles, all of which had to be beaten back, and it was rife with contention, much of it playing out in a long series of very public lawsuits and legal roadblocks, not to mention heaps of public scorn. Many in Abilene would fight tooth and nail to keep Perkins from creating a town. Others prayed for divine intervention. The three year struggle was snared in constant and protracted legal battles, landing twice on the steps of the Texas Supreme Court.

Such complications, contempt and tribulations would have daunted a lesser man. Even by his opponents, Perkins was seen as audacious and his idea as boldly ambitious, one that would require undaunted determination in order to pull it off. Dallas Perkins was just that — undaunted and quite determined.

The turkey farm purchased by Dallas and Nancy Perkins was set along Elm Creek, just east of the old Anson Highway and only 500 yards from Abilene's northern city limit. Downtown Abilene was three and a half miles away. The family moved from their home on North 21st Street and into a two-story house on the farm property. There was a barn out back of the house and, although Dallas Perkins had no intention of raising turkeys, the barn might very well have been the real reason he picked up and moved. In the back of his mind, he thought it might make a nice liquor store.

Within the boundaries of Impact were seventy homes, with just fifty-five occupied. The residents were best described as economically disadvantaged and they were living in a location prone to flooding from the nearby creek. In 1956 the residents petitioned for the area to be annexed into Abilene in order to receive city services, but the city commissioners turned down the request due to the possible expense related to flooding. It was a decision the City of Abilene would come to deeply regret.

Soon, Perkins was visiting the scattered neighbors and offering them cash for a future right to buy their homes. Many took him up on the option and agreed with his plan to create a new town. After all, since Abilene had rejected them, maybe creating their own city was the best way to control their destiny. When a reporter asked Perkins why he and the petitioners were looking to incorporate their own municipality, he replied, "Area residents are interested in securing conveniences which are not now offered by Abilene."

1960

Only months after moving to the turkey farm, the first move in the chess game took place. On the morning of

February 1, 1960, Perkins and his coffee-drinking friend, attorney Dan Sorrells, presented to Taylor County Judge Reed Ingalsbe a petition signed by twenty-nine residents living within the proposed borders of Impact seeking to hold an election to decide if they would incorporate as their own town. Ingalsbe checked over the paperwork, found everything in order, and approved the request. He then appointed Perkins as the election judge and issued an order for the vote to take place less than two weeks later, on Saturday, February 13. Ingalsbe then went out of town for four days.

The day after Ingalsbe approved the petition, Abilene city commissioners (Note: commissioners were renamed as councilmen and councilwomen in 1963) met in an emergency session regarding the "bombshell proposal." It seemed all of Abilene suspected that if Impact became a legally incorporated city, then a handful of that town's citizens would next petition for a local option election and vote to sell beer, wine and nasty old whiskey right on the very doorstep of Abilene.

Abilene city commissioners and the city manager discussed a variety of options to head off the plan. In the event they could not stop things, and the tiny hamlet did in fact vote wet, commissioners even discussed closing Abilene streets connected to Impact, reasoning that folks can't buy liquor if they can't get to it. But the best option seemed for Abilene to immediately do what it had not done earlier — annex the property — thus turning the Impact landowners into Abilene citizens and Abilene voters. Two days before the scheduled election to incorporate Impact, Abilene commissioners opted to immediately annex a parcel just north of Abilene that included the Impact area. (In order to forestall others from carrying out a similar scheme, the city also annexed the area around Kirby Lake and an area south of Abilene known as Wylie.)

When Judge Ingalsbe returned from out of town, he was met with a firestorm. In his words, "a great controversy had arisen." He faced growing pressure to reverse course and rescind his earlier election order. Much of the arm-twisting came from his friends and the Abilene Ministerial Alliance who hoped to stop Perkins. Ingalsbe, a member and deacon of University Baptist Church, quickly convened a public hearing on the matter to hear from both sides. The City of Abilene was represented by attorney Tom Eplen, while Dan Sorrells argued for Impact. The hearing provided Ingalsbe with cover for placating the Ministerial Alliance, allowing him to reconsider the issue and toss out his earlier order. He later admitted he had decided before the hearing to revoke approval for the election in Impact but knew he had to go through the motions. Ingalsbe wanted no part, and no future blame, in making it possible for a saloon — or worse, a city that was one big saloon — to pop up in Taylor County. He longed to sit guilt-free in his pew on Sunday.

Forty-eight hours before the vote, Ingalsbe announced his decision to cancel his previous order, saying the Impact area "does not have visible means of support to function as a city and that it is part of the larger Abilene community." His action set in motion a lawsuit that would wind its way to the Texas Supreme Court.

Despite Ingalsbe pulling the plug, Perkins decided to go ahead and hold the election as scheduled on Saturday, February 13. The polling site was Perkins' living room. The election was a landslide. The vote to incorporate passed unanimously, 27-0. Perkins quipped, "I thought it was a very good turnout."

On Monday morning, Perkins and Sorrells brought the lone ballot box to the courthouse for Ingalsbe to canvass the results and officially declare Impact as a new Texas municipality. Ingalsbe refused to certify the election since he had canceled it two days earlier. He also denied reimbursement of election expenses totaling $43. The Impact ballot box was locked in the county vault until things could be sorted out. That would take a while.

Perkins immediately sought a court order to force Judge Ingalsbe to canvass the votes and declare that Taylor County, indeed, had a new little town. The ensuing legal battle was full of twists and turns, providing highs and lows for both sides. Although legally styled as "Perkins v. Ingalsbe," for all practical reasons it was "Abilene v. Impact."

Perkins lost in Abilene's 42nd district court when judge J.R. Black Sr. upheld Ingalsbe's action. Perkins then went to the 11th Court of Civil Appeals in Eastland, where he lost again. His final recourse was to appeal to the Texas Supreme Court. A third strike there would end his hopes of creating

Impact. However, his chances of getting a hit and winning a reversal from the state's high court improved greatly when an old family friend came to visit.

Thomas "Pinkie" Roden of Odessa was a walking contradiction — described by newspaper writer Mike Cochran as "a civic godfather with a dark side and a shadowy past." Despite a criminal history, including a stint in prison, in his later years Pinkie reinvented himself. Known as the "Wizard of the West," he would twice be named National Retailer of the Year and was honored as Odessa's outstanding citizen in 1976. No less than former Texas Governor Preston Smith claimed that Pinkie was one of the top ten people he knew.

Roden was born in 1911, the second of six children born to Arthur and Allie Roden in Chalk Mountain, a small community in Erath County. Arthur Roden was a druggist and lay leader in the Primitive Baptist Church. At the age of sixteen, Pinkie dropped out of school in Glen Rose and moved to Fort Worth where he learned the bootlegging business. During Prohibition he became the largest supplier of liquor in West Texas and maintained his lead position by elbowing out any upstart competition. With the repeal of Prohibition in 1933, Pinkie became the largest legal retailer of alcohol in that same area while remaining as the bootleg supplier to counties that remained dry, including Taylor County. Over time, Pinkie Roden became one of America's top ten purveyors of alcohol.

Before the repeal of Prohibition, Pinkie managed

to stay one step ahead of the law, in part due to hiring outstanding attorneys. The Abilene firm of Cunningham and Oliver — J.F. Cunningham and his brother-in-law Bruce Oliver — handled many of Pinkie's legal entanglements. Cunningham's son, Oliver, joined the firm after serving in World War I and became well-acquainted with Pinkie as he helped him maneuver around a variety of legal hurdles. And, it would be Oliver Cunningham's daughter, Nancy, who would marry Dallas Perkins. Pinkie sent a wedding gift.

The *Abilene Reporter-News* named Impact as the number one news story in 1960.

1961

When fifty-year-old Pinkie Roden showed up at the home of Dallas and Nancy Perkins in 1961, he certainly did not arrive as a stranger. He came as a friend, and he came to offer a trade. At his expense, Pinkie would provide high-powered legal help to argue the case of Impact before the state Supreme Court, offering to employ the Austin law firm of Cofer and Cofer to handle the appeal, even hinting that all would likely turn out in favor of Impact. John Cofer was a powerhouse in Texas legal matters, and Pinkie was a longtime client. Cofer had represented Lyndon B. Johnson in 1948 when LBJ and the state Democratic Party were accused of ballot-rigging in the primary race for the U.S. Senate seat, a bitter battle that possibly played a part in Impact's application for liquor licenses fourteen years later. (Cofer also represented famed swindler Billie Sol Estes.) In return for Pinkie providing Cofer's services to Perkins, Pinkie would need something in return — a liquor store in Impact.

When the case came before the Supreme Court in March 1961, it was John Cofer sitting beside and advising Dan Sorrells as he made the oral arguments on behalf of Dallas Perkins. The high court issued its judgment on June 14, 1961, nearly a year and a half after the election to incorporate Impact. And, just as Pinkie predicted, things turned out in favor of Perkins. By a vote of 8-1, the Court overturned the appellate ruling in Dallas G. Perkins v. Reed Ingalsbe and directed the 42nd District judge to order Ingalsbe to canvass those twenty-seven ballots. That same day, the courthouse custodian inadvertently hoisted the U.S. flag upside down on the courthouse flagpole — the international signal of distress — aptly capturing the feelings of many in Abilene.

Just after 9 a.m. on August 2, 1961, the dusty ballot box from the Impact election was removed from the Taylor County vault. Taylor County Judge Ingalsbe then carried out the court order as he counted the ballots and proclaimed that the election held in February 1960 seemed to "all be in perfect order." After signing the papers officially creating Impact, Ingalsbe said, "Well, I feel just like General Robert E. Lee at Appomattox." He then added, "We now have a new city in Taylor County." Ingalsbe next set an election date so the new citizens of Impact could return to the polls to elect a mayor, town marshal and aldermen.

The day after the mayoral election, the *Abilene Reporter-*

News reported the results and, for the first time, carried a dateline of "IMPACT, TX." Running unopposed, Dallas Perkins was elected mayor after twenty citizens voted for him and, with sixteen votes, his wife Nancy won a spot as the town marshal and later filled the position of city secretary. Mayor Perkins issued his first official statement, "I pledge that as long as I am mayor of Impact I will never squander this city's money fighting any smaller city trying to incorporate in any nearby location, as some of our neighbors have done."

Tom Eplen, the attorney representing Abilene, claimed that the close proximity of Impact was a threat to the orderly growth of Abilene and vowed to continue to fight, hoping to nullify the creation of the new neighbor. Impact mayor Perkins told his newly elected aldermen that Abilene's efforts to undo the incorporation of Impact was forcing the infant town to increase city funds in order to fight back. And the most logical way for Impact to raise such revenue would be for the citizens to consider a local option election, allowing the town to collect sales tax on alcohol. Such a move, he added, would also provide funds to pave the streets, pick up the trash and provide other services, negating the need to directly tax the people of Impact.

Three weeks after becoming a bona fide Texas city, the fear of many Abilenians materialized when mayor Perkins returned to the Taylor County courthouse, this time to file an application for a petition seeking to hold an election for approving the off-premises sale of alcoholic beverages. The required number of signatures to trigger the setting of an election was one-fourth of voters casting ballots in the most recent city election; that came out to five people. Perkins secured the required signatures by lunchtime. Taylor County commissioners set September 18, 1961, as the date for the local option election in Impact. Before election day, Impact applied for a second election, this one to approve sales of on-premises consumption of alcohol. That vote was set for October 2, barely two weeks after the off-premises election. A handful of northern Taylor County residents stood poised to reshape the Abilene culture. That did not sit well with Abilene city commissioners, who vowed to legally challenge the validity of Impact. It also didn't sit well with a lot of Abilenians who organized to fight back.

Like the year before, the *Abilene Reporter-News* named Impact as the number one news story in 1961.

1962

Abilene's largest congregation, First Baptist Church, was integral in forming an organized group known as Citizens for a Better Taylor County (CBTC), whose purpose was to oppose alcohol sales. The Perkinses just so happened to be members of First Baptist.

The membership of CBTC totalled more than 800 and included many well-known Abilene citizens. Officers included Chuck Moser, the school district's athletic coordinator and famed Abilene High football coach, along with Crutcher Scott and Garvin Beauchamp of Abilene Christian College, and a longtime First Baptist deacon and future county commissioner Bert Chapman. The group quickly formulated a plan to pressure the state legislature to void the validation of Impact. Another goal was to pressure the administrator of the state's Liquor Control Board to delay issuance of any liquor permits for Impact.

On election day, Impact voters favored off-premise consumption 18-2. Fourteen days later, they returned to the polls, approving on-premise consumption 17-4. The former turkey barn was already being renovated into a liquor store.

The City of Abilene took legal action, challenging the validity of the incorporation of Impact, claiming that Perkins did not incorporate a town but "only an arbitrary slice of a town." This time, 42nd District Court Judge J.R. Black Sr. sided with Perkins. Abilene appealed to the 11th Court of Civil Court of Appeals in Eastland.

Meanwhile, three applicants filed for licenses to operate a package store in Impact. One was submitted by C.C.H. Inc. controlled by Roden, a second one from Columbia Liquors Inc., and the third from Roy Jackson of San Angelo, who was negotiating with Perkins for an Impact building to lease. But with the appeal pending before the Eastland court, Liquor Control Board administrator Coke Stevenson Jr. refused to issue any permits. (According to some, it was highly likely that Stevenson's real motivation to impede Impact liquor sales was rooted in a personal grudge. Coke Stevenson Jr. was the son of the former Texas governor who had lost the

1948 Democratic Party primary for the U.S. Senate to Lyndon
Johnson. The "rigged" primary election cost Stevenson's
dad the Senate seat nomination by eighty-seven votes. With
Johnson's attorney John Cofer now playing a role in the
creation of Impact, Stevenson was in no rush to do anything
to help Cofer or his clients.)

With Stevenson refusing to issue a license for his Impact
store, Pinkie Roden applied some force by instructing
his Abilene attorney, Beverly Tarpley, to petition Odessa
District Court Judge Claude Milburn to force Stevenson to
grant the package store permit to C.C.H. Inc. Once again the
11th Court of Civil Appeals stepped in, issuing an injunction
barring Milburn from forcing Stevenson to act until the court
ruled on the legal challenge to the incorporation of Impact.
When an Ector County deputy served Judge Milburn with
the injunction, he shot back, "The injunction only denies me
the right to make a decision. It doesn't deny me the right to
hear the petition." He went ahead and let Tarpley state the
case for C.C.H. to get its permit from Stevenson.

The Eastland court overturned Black's decision, ruling
that, in fact, Impact was not legally incorporated, that it had
been done so "by the whim and caprice of Mr. Perkins." On
behalf of Perkins, attorney John Cofer quickly applied to the
Texas Supreme Court for a writ of error, i.e. for the Court of
Appeals to send the case to the high court for review. And on
Wednesday, December 19, 1962, the Supreme Court agreed
to hear Perkin's plea that the Eastland court had erred.

The Supreme Court's willingness to consider the case

opened the door for Impact liquor sales to take another
step forward. On Thursday, Odessa judge Claude Milburn
ruled on the earlier petition, compelling administrator Coke
Stevenson Jr. to issue the package store permit for C.C.H.
Stevenson went ahead and signed off on permits for Columbia
and Roy Jackson to also operate package stores in Impact. By
7 p.m. Friday the first truckload of liquor arrived in Impact
from Pinkie's warehouse in Odessa. The truck backed up to
the rear of C.C.H. package store, and began unloading boxes
of whiskey. When asked if Pinkie owned the store, manager
John McCown parsed his answer, saying that Roden was not
a stockholder. But, standing nearby, watching the activity,
was Pinkie Roden.

Also on Friday, the City of Abilene made a last ditch
effort to stop things, asking the Texas Supreme Court to
issue an injunction to halt the opening of package stores in
Impact. The court held that it had no authority to grant such
an order.

Late Friday night Impact mayor Perkins hired a four-
man police force to keep law and order once the anticipated
crowds began to arrive.

And they came. Three days before Christmas 1962, at 9
a.m., the C.C.H. liquor store opened for business. The first
person to legally buy a bottle of whiskey in Taylor County in
sixty years was Dallas Perkins. Behind him was a long line
of Abilenians, cash in hand, queuing up at one of the four
registers, while outside it was bumper-to-bumper traffic as
hundreds arrived in Impact.

A Dallas television station reported that $25,000 ($260,000 in 2024 dollars) worth of alcohol was sold that first day. One customer remarked that it was "the first alcohol I ever bought in Taylor County that involved a cash register." Another lifelong Abilenian walked into the store and said, "Oh my! I've never seen so much whiskey so close to Abilene in my life!"

The second store, operated by Columbia Liquors, began selling from the converted barn behind Perkins' home. Pinkie and Perkins sought to mask their respective ownership in C.C.H. Inc. and in Columbia Liquors, knowing that the anti-alcohol crowd in Abilene would proclaim the two had conspired all along to make money off of alcohol sales from the incorporation of Impact. (The third license was never used. Roy Jackson of San Angelo and Perkins could not come to terms for Jackson to lease a building.)

In the first week, the two stores grossed nearly $100,000 ($1,000,000 in 2024). The City of Impact was set to receive a tax of one and a half percent on all sales.

On January 16, 1963, Texas Supreme Court judges listened to seventy-five minutes of arguments in the appeal of the lower court's invalidation of the incorporation of Impact. Tom Eplen, representing Abilene, argued to uphold the ruling, while John Cofer pressed the court to recognize Impact as a legally incorporated city. If the court upheld the Eastland court ruling then Impact would fail to exist, resulting in the closing of the newly-opened liquor stores. But, if the court was swayed by Cofer and overturned the lower court ruling, then Impact would be deemed a city and could continue to supply Abilene with alcohol. Perkins was not in the courtroom, but Abilene attorney Beverly Tarpley, the legal representative of Pinkie's C.C.H. Inc., sat listening to the proceedings.

The court handed down its decision in April 1963, ruling 7-2 that Impact was legally incorporated and, at long last, putting the question to rest. The banner headline in the Abilene paper screamed: IMPACT RULED LEGAL CITY.

Despite more than three years of social pressure and legal and political maneuvering, neither the Abilene commissioners nor the Citizens for a Better Taylor County could stop the sale of alcohol in Impact. But within days Abilene annexed all the land surrounding Impact.

Just two package stores would operate in Impact, one owned by Pinkie Roden and one owned by Dallas Perkins. Perkins also owned a small grocery store, Impact Food Mart, which could sell beer on Sundays. In the first month, sales at the three outlets totaled $463,000, just shy of $5 million in 2024 purchasing power.

Abilenians arrived in droves, buying whiskey and other libations. However, since beer required a separate state license, you could not grab a six-pack until May 31, 1963, and even then you could not buy it cold. Perkins and Pinkie astutely offered no ice cold beer at Impact, reasoning that if you had a frosty Bud in the front seat, then, on your drive back into Abilene, you just might drink it. You might even finish it and, perhaps, toss the empty bottle out the window and onto an Abilene lawn. Or, worse get pulled over with an open bottle of Impact beer fouling the Abilene aroma.

For the third year in a row the *Abilene Reporter-News* named Impact as the number one news story.

1963

For the year of 1963, total sales amounted to $2.5 million — or $25 million in 2024 dollars. Abilene police chief Warren Dodson reported that Impact made little difference in law enforcement, noting "there has been no difference to speak of since Impact." Dodson told a reporter that in the fifteen months prior to Impact opening for business, there were 2,190 arrests in Abilene for drunkenness and 305 persons arrested for driving while intoxicated. For the year of 1963, with Impact open for business, both were down — arrests for public drunkenness were 2,171 and there were 239 DWIs. The district supervisor for the Liquor Control Board, Loyd Owen, reported that bootlegging arrests dropped 75 percent, adding, "The full-time bootlegger is now non-existent in Abilene and the only ones operating are those selling from their hip pockets." Taylor County bootleggers had dwindled from a high of around 250 in 1960 to just a handful by the end of 1966.

Liquor stores located within forty-five miles of Abilene saw sales plummet. In Stamford, the Party Port reported that sales were off by 75 percent. The same occurred at Cecil's Beer in the tiny community of Tuxedo in neighboring Jones

County, but there was little concern — it was owned by Pinkie Roden.

By March 1963 Impact tax revenue funded the paving of eleven blocks and the installation of street lights. Some Abilene residents complained that one street leading into Impact was raising dust from all the traffic. So Impact covered the cost of spreading oil on the Abilene street to keep the dust down.

Tiny Impact held a virtual liquor monopoly in Taylor County from December 1962 until 1978, or at least had the lion's share of sales. On December 7, 1965, voters in Buffalo Gap came to the school gymnasium to cast their votes in a local option election, with some hoping their town could gain tax revenue just like Impact. Gappers approved the on-premises sale of beer and off-premises sale of all alcoholic beverages, but just barely — the vote was 77-76.

Buffalo Gap restricted its wet zone to an eleven acre tract on the south end of town. Six months after the election, Zentner's Steakhouse opened there, followed by a German biergarten known as Deutschlander Garten that operated across the street. You could have a frosty beer with your steak or schnitzel. By July, an application had been made for a liquor store as well. The store was built with two front doors and a partition separating the space inside. One door led to a regular package store that, by state law, had to close each night at 10 p.m. and could not operate on Sundays, while the other door led to a space licensed to sell beer and wine, which state law allowed to remain open until a later hour and on Sundays — one building to offer any and all intoxicants for any hour of the day as allowed by the State of Texas. The group putting in the store was from Odessa, the hometown of Pinkie Roden.

Perkins resisted putting in a bar or restaurant at Impact, something many in Abilene felt certain he would do, which very well could have been the reason he didn't. In Buffalo Gap, where restaurants sold beer over the bar, they could operate on Sunday, and many Abilenians adopted a weekend habit of making the leisurely twelve-mile drive south in order to have a steak and a beer in Buffalo Gap.

Two other Taylor County towns made a run at capitalizing on legal alcohol sales. In 1964, voters in Tye went to the polls but soundly defeated such sales, 190-66. Two years later they tried again, coming up short once more, 181-64. And in 1966, voters in the south Taylor County town of Lawn turned down alcohol sales, 112-62.

Following the establishment of Impact and the availability of liquid refreshment in Buffalo Gap, a detente seemed to settle over Abilene. Those opposed to alcohol were content knowing that the innocent youth of Abilene did not have to see beer and wine out in the open. While those looking to buy beer and wine were not overly bothered by making a short drive to buy it.

So for the rest of the 1960s and early '70s the state of affairs maintained a chilled equilibrium. Dallas Perkins never dreamed his idea would last forever, but he also never thought it would last as long as it did. In a 2024 interview,

Dallas Perkins Jr., son of the Impact founder, said, "The alcohol monopoly shared by Perkins and Pinkie Roden prospered much longer than they imagined. They assumed that once Abilene realized the amount of tax revenue they were giving up, the citizenry would vote the town wet." The two liquor store owners hoped to make hay while the sun was shining, never expecting it to shine for sixteen years.

What is wet on both ends and dry in the middle?
Abilene.

1976: Round One

1975

The fragile truce between Wets and Drys began to fray in September 1975. A group of twenty-six Abilenians announced they intended to apply for a countywide local option election. The group called itself the Abilene Committee on Taxation and Trade, or ACTT. The chairman of ACTT was Abilene attorney W.L. "Dub" Burke Jr. who held a press conference just before noon at a new sandwich shop on Chestnut Street called the Hangin' Tree and owned by Burke's firm. Burke pointed out, "We have liquor in Abilene, shutting our eyes to the issue will not make it go away. The issue seems clear enough. It is not a 'wet versus dry' issue but whether or not the City of Abilene will be able to collect tax dollars on the liquor industry that already operates within our city limits." He then added, "Naturally, we foresee strong opposition."

A week later ACTT — now backed by thirty-five citizens

— filed a formal application with the Taylor County clerk
requesting an election. ACTT had thirty days to secure
4,100 voter signatures and get the proposal on the ballot.
Burke picked up 500 copies of the petition from Taylor
County Clerk Mrs. Chester Hutcheson, and ACTT quickly
got to work spreading them all across town: at River Oaks
Shopping Center, Westgate, all Colonial Food Stores, at Bill's
Drive-In on Barrow, at Skaggs-Albertsons on South 14th, and
at all of the Skinny's convenience stores. ACTT also planned
to send out volunteers to collect signatures door to door. The
group hired a Fort Worth public relations firm to help with
the effort.

Two days after the filing, the opposition girded for battle.
A newspaper ad paid for by Highland Church of Christ
cautioned, "Your name will be a matter of public record if
you sign the petition." Days later, forty congregations of
the Abilene Baptist Association took out an ad serving up
a similar warning: "We would like our friends who are
promoting a possible election to know that every name on
the proposed election petition will be printed in a double
page ad of the *Abilene Reporter-News*." And they tossed in
a side dish of admonition , "True, alcohol is available in our
city on a private club or 'back door' basis. Why make it a
'public' or 'front door' business at the cost of destroying one
of the most unique cities in Texas?" Burke responded, "We
understand their views and appreciate them. We don't fault
them for standing up for what they believe in." Others said
the threat to name names of the petitioners was bullying and

smacked of blackmail.

The opposition took on a more structured strategy when a group of Drys formed an organization known as Citizens for a Better Community (CBC). It was headed up by local businessman Robert Gooch. Abilene clergy and university leaders lined up firmly behind CBC efforts. One Abilene pastor noted, "Abilene is wet now, sure, but I don't think it should become wetter."

After five days of circulating the petitions, ACTT announced it had more than half of the necessary signatures. A complaint by one door-to-door volunteer aptly described the growing divide. In a letter to the editor she wrote that many homeowners slammed their doors in her face or preached sermons at her. She requested, "So please, all of you Christians, use a little kindness by answering yes or no instead of hateful no's and slamming doors."

Nine days before the deadline, approximately 700 petitions containing nearly twice the required number of signatures were filed by ACTT with the county clerk. The members of the Baptist Association backed down and voted to not print the names in the newspaper.

However, the whole matter was thrown off track when district attorney Ed Paynter advised the county clerk to not approve ACTT's petition due to a quirk in the law which affected Abilene. Because the city was not contained within one county — part of Abilene, around Lake Fort Phantom Hill, is in Jones county — and state law prohibited local option elections for cities whose boundaries spanned more

than one county. The county clerk followed the advice of
Paynter and denied ACTT's request. CBC breathed a sigh of
relief. But not for long.

Undaunted, ACTT quickly filed for a local option liquor
election in Precinct 1 of Taylor County, which included
approximately ninety-five percent of the Abilene population
and around eighty-five percent of city territory, and excluded
the Jones County portion. The whole petition process had
to begin anew. Signatures would again need to be secured
from qualified voters, but now only from those residing in
Precinct 1.

Thirteen days after refiling, ACTT turned in a second
set of signatures. This time the county clerk approved the
petition. The local option election for Precinct 1 was set for
February 17, 1976. In the meantime, both Wets and Drys
collected money and launched media campaigns to sway the
voting public.

1976

The CBC raked in $11,690 while ACTT reported $33,909
was in its coffers, including two loans totaling $16,000
guaranteed by a group of nineteen ACTT backers, including
Burke and Abilene restaurateur Mack Eplen. Predictably,
letters to the editor on the subject picked up. One asked,
"If Jesus had lived in Abilene, would he have turned the
water into Kool-Aid?" A CBC ad read, "So, we'll have fine
restaurants, more tourists, lower taxes. How about Skid
Row? More winos, more visual pollution, DWI's and traffic

carnage, scars on the land and on the spirit of our people."
ACTT ran an ad asking its own question, "Who should
collect taxes on Abilene liquor? Impact or Abilene?"

Another anti-alcohol group, known as the Taylor
County Committee for the Protection of Our Children,
took out full-page ads suggesting that a "yes" vote would
mean "more winos, go-go dancers, honky tonks and bar
brawls." ACTT countered with an ad headlined, "Hysteria
vs Logic" highlighting that there were already forty-three
"private clubs" where drink was available in Abilene. And
to punctuate its p.r. effort, ACTT lined up a California sky-
writer to spell "VOTE WET" in the skies over Abilene on
election day. (Windy conditions scrapped the last minute
advertising stunt.)

The weather seemed to foretell what the day held. A
dust storm blew through town, highlighting the existing
dry conditions as more than 24,000 voters headed to the
polls. Early results showed the contest to be nip and tuck,
but late in the evening two of the last election boxes came
in. Box 45, which had been set up in a corridor of Abilene
Christian's Moody Coliseum, recorded only 89 voters opting
"wet" while a whopping 589 chose to keep things dry. Box
14, nearest to Hardin-Simmons University, voted 2.5 to 1 in
favor of banning alcohol sales. The lopsided returns from the
university boxes put the Drys over the top. When the final
election results were announced at the HSU v. Centenary
basketball game being played at the Taylor County Coliseum,
the largely Baptist crowd provided a prolonged ovation.

Few were more interested in the election outcome than Impact mayor Dallas Perkins. With the results still unofficial, a high wind blew down a power line that put Perkins' home in the dark. He went to bed unaware that Impact's monopoly remained intact.

The final vote showed that 12,905 were in favor of keeping Abilene dry, while 11,291 hoped to live in a wet city. The difference was 1,614. Dick Tarpley, managing editor of the *Abilene Reporter-News*, felt the overall outcome might have gone the other way without the college boxes; Baptist and Church of Christ voters ended the 1976 push for legal alcohol. The day after the election, Associated Press reporter Mike Cochran phoned Dallas Perkins for his thoughts on the election outcome. He replied, "What election? Was today the day they voted? How'd it come out?"

I just want them to shut up about it.

I don't care whether it goes wet or dry.

Abilene's been the wettest dry town around anyhow.

Lila Binkley

1978: Round Two

Ahead of the 1976 election, Walter Dawkins, an Abilene Christian University sophomore basketball player, told a reporter, "I may get kicked out (of ACU) for saying this, but I don't feel anyone has the right to say what I do with my private life." Now, two years later, senior Dawkins learned that his college had quite a say in his private life. The 6'1" starting guard was suspended from the basketball squad for the remainder of his final season. Dawkins was not suspended due to his 1976 comments; rather, he committed an unforgivable transgression in February 1978. Dawkins had delivered an ACU basketball team poster to a local business to display the upcoming schedule and drum up support for Wildcat basketball. However, ACU rules prohibited any student from entering an establishment selling alcoholic

beverages; Dawkins had delivered the poster to the private
Upstairs Club on Oak Street — an establishment that most
assuredly sold alcoholic beverages. The school's athletic
director, Wally Bullington, suspended Dawkins from the
team, then saw to it that the team poster was removed from
the club.

1978

Following the Drys victory in 1976, the push for a new
election began to take shape fairly soon. By law, a second
local option election could not take place until twelve months
had passed. So, fourteen months later, in April 1978, a new
push began. This time, a group called Update '78 formed
with the stated purpose "to seek the legal sale of all alcoholic
beverages including mixed beverages in Justice Precinct
Number 1, Taylor County, Texas, through promotion of such
purpose in a local option liquor election."

This time, Dub Burke opted to stay on the sidelines.
The new effort was led by local oilman Pat Dunigan and
Mel Richards, president of Midstates Oil and a co-owner of
the Sheraton Inn on Pine Street. Richards filed a document
naming himself as treasurer of a political campaign — a state
requirement before contributions could be accepted.

Within weeks a reactivated Citizens for a Better
Community set out to once again push back the effort to
make Abilene wet. This time the CBC was led by oral surgeon
Dr. Robert Strader along with ACU director of planning

Neil Fry. Abilene city councilman Emil Ogden threw his support behind the CBC saying, "No one has convinced me that increased (alcohol) outlets will create Utopia on the Catclaw," adding that he did not like the idea of his daughter "being confronted by beer purchasers when she goes to a drive-in grocery to buy an Icee."

Other leaders in the CBC included ACU's Wally Bullington and school vice president Garvin Beauchamp, along with the pastors of the city's two largest Baptist congregations, Dr. James Flamming of First Baptist and Jack Ridlehoover of Pioneer Drive Baptist Church.

Update '78 filed an application for petitions requesting the county clerk to call an election. The request was signed by eighty-three Abilenians, many of whom backed the failed 1976 effort. Update '78 needed to collect 4,356 signatures to get a measure approving the sale of all alcoholic beverages on the ballot. On the same day, a second group, known as Citizens for Moderation — seeking a vote on mixed drinks only, not retail sales of beer and wine — filed for an election petition. Citizens for Moderation were seen as pro-Impact since they were not pushing for Abilene to have retail beer and wine outlets. Ironically, the leader of Citizens for Moderation was former district attorney Ed Paynter, who had represented the county in the 1976 election and endeared himself to those opposed to alcohol. However, his personal opinion on the sale of alcohol was now clear.

Petitions for Update '78 were printed on gold paper, while Citizens for Moderation used white paper. On May

5, Update '78 turned in its gold petitions with more than 6,000 names listed. Citizens for Moderation failed to secure enough signatures within the thirty day deadline.

Based on the request submitted by Update '78, County Judge Roy Skaggs and the four county commissioners set the election for Saturday, June 17, 1978.

As the day approached, many felt compelled to state their convictions by sending a letter to the editor, including the aforementioned state inmate Larry Legg and the youth group at Trinity Baptist Church.

Of the 52,000 voters registered in Precinct 1, nearly 50 percent turned out to make their wishes known. The paper ballot had two choices – "FOR the legal sale of all alcoholic beverages including mixed beverages" or "AGAINST" the same. Awkwardly, voters were instructed to "scratch or mark out one statement so that the one remaining indicates the way you wish to vote." So, don't mark your wish, instead mark through the option you did not want.

On the day of the election, a newspaper reporter approached Abilenian Jerry Adams, who was loading beer in his truck outside the Impact Food Mart, and asked him about the election taking place. Adams aptly noted, "We're just fooling ourselves, calling it a dry town."

The election results would be known that night, but it would not be the end of things; in fact, it was just the beginning. The ensuing battle of wills, held in a variety of courtrooms, extended the legal outcome for months and, along the way, divided Abilene as never before.

The banner headline of the *Abilene Reporter-News* the morning after the election screamed "Wets Win By a Drop." The unofficial vote margin was razor-thin — out of the 23,086 ballots cast, the Wets outpolled the Drys by a mere 131 votes. Dry forces tallied 49.73 percent, the Wets passed the threshold at 50.27 percent. Early on, the Drys grabbed a razor thin lead when absentee votes showed they had a 13-vote advantage. By 7:30 p.m., with fourteen southside boxes counted, things had swung the other direction; Wets showed a lead by more than 1,000 votes. But by 8 p.m. that margin disappeared as the ACU precinct boxes came in, showing that they favored remaining dry by 85 percent. Box 45, the ACU Moody Coliseum box, again turned in a dry majority, as did Box 11 located at the ACU Fire Station. However, the Dyess Air Force Base precinct provided 725 votes for liquor sales and only 226 against, helping to tip things in favor of the Wets. (On the day of the 1976 vote, Dyess was on base alert, preventing many from reaching their voting location.)

An added factor in the Wet victory was the date. June was summertime, and many Abilene college students and faculty were not in the city on election day. CBC secretary Neil Fry asserted, "If the students had been here, there is no question the outcome would have been different."

Ironically, the box which became the determining factor in a Wet victory, Box 19, was the Wylie box. Wylie was only part of Abilene because, eighteen years earlier, it had been annexed into Abilene as the city commissioners sought to keep that population from voting to separately incorporate as Impact had done.

With the margin of victory so thin — less than half of one percent — the CBC immediately said it would seek a recount.

But, first things first. For the election results to become official, the commissioners court had to canvass the votes, certify that all was correct, and officially accept the results into its minutes. The county commissioners court was composed of five people — Taylor County Judge Roy Skaggs and the four commissioners, including Bert Chapman (an earlier officer in the organized effort to stop Impact) who represented Precinct 1. The other commissioners were Joe McDuff, Felton Saverance and Jake McMillon. A tie vote, on any matter, by the four commissioners would be broken by a vote from Judge Skaggs.

Six days after the election, the court met to canvass the results. But by a 3-2 vote the court recessed before tallying the votes. Judge Skaggs and commissioners Chapman and McDuff wanted to ask the Texas attorney general for an opinion on whether or not the commissioners court could order a recount. The trio voted for the postponement despite the advice being offered by the court's own legal counsel. Assistant District Attorney Gary Hacker, who had been appointed by District Attorney Lynn Ingalsbe to be the legal advisor to the court, repeatedly told the group that "the law made no provision authorizing a recount in a special election in which paper ballots were used and when there was no candidate on the ballot." After Skaggs, McDuff and

Chapman ignored Hacker's advice, Hacker requested to be relieved of his position as legal counsel to the court. Ingalsbe did not relieve him of the duty, but since Hacker was heading on vacation, Ingalsbe took on the responsibility himself and let it be known that he agreed with Hacker's advice — the commissioners court had no authority to call for a recount. Regardless, Skaggs instructed Ingalsbe to submit the question to the state Attorney General for an opinion. (Lynn Ingalsbe's father, Reed, had been the county judge eighteen years earlier during the Impact drama.)

The attorney representing Update '78, C.G. Whitten, quickly filed a motion in the 42nd District Court seeking a writ of mandamus, or an order commanding the commissioners to canvass the election results. Judge Don Lane set the hearing for Friday, July 14.

The eleven days stretching from Monday, July 10, to Thursday, July 20, were unlike any in the history of Abilene. For one thing, it was stiflingly hot. A heat wave had kept the city sweltering since July 1 when the daily high temperature broke the 100 mark. But the hot weather outside was surpassed by the fervency flaring up inside the Taylor County courthouse. Over those eleven days, tempers reached the boiling point. Abilene did not emerge from seventy-five years of prohibition without a blistering fight.

The attorney general's ruling on the legal standing for the commissioners to call a recount was expected on July 10.

MONDAY, JULY 10

For the tenth day in a row, Abilenians sweated under triple digit temperatures. The change of command ceremony at Dyess had to be moved from the parade ground to an indoor recreation hall to escape the scorching sun and avoid having participants pass out.

The regularly scheduled Monday meeting of the commissioners court was standing room only. Many had come to witness the historic moment. If all went as expected, Abilene would be officially wet by lunch. Instead, everyone present was stunned when the exact opposite took place.

Judge Skaggs called the meeting to order. The first item on the agenda was the canvassing of the votes from the June 17 election. District Attorney Ingalsbe reported that he had spoken with state Attorney General John Hill who advised that the commissioners had no legal standing to order a recount, thus reinforcing what the commissioners had been told by their legal counsel, Gary Hacker, two and a half weeks earlier.

With the recount question put to rest, the commissioners began to canvass the votes, tallying the results from each ballot box to ensure they matched the signed results turned in by the election judges. However, when they got to the votes cast in Precinct 19 — encompassing much of the Wylie area — Skaggs set those results aside. After counting and checking all the other precinct tallies, Skaggs told the commissioners that Box 19 needed to be excluded from the count due to "a serious, obvious legal question" concerning the boundaries of that voting precinct. With all boxes counted, except Box 19, the Drys were in the lead.

The legal question Skaggs was referring to pertained to a recent annexation by the City of Abilene (unrelated to the 1960 annexation) that caused a portion of voting Precinct 19 to lie partially in two justice precincts. Skaggs said, "It seems to me we can't canvass the results of Precinct 19." Update '78 attorney C.G. Whitten leapt to his feet, "I think you have to!" He pointed out that the court had no authority to involve itself in legal matters but only to canvass the total. Even the Austin attorney representing the CBC, Randall "Buck" Wood, agreed — the commissioners could not exclude a box. District Attorney Ingalsbe interjected, asking Skaggs, "Do you want to hear my opinion or do you just want to take for granted what my opinion is?" Before waiting for an answer Ingalsbe added, "There is no legal problem involving Precinct 19." He pointed out that the change in the city limits due to the annexation did not affect the precinct boundaries. At the point of exasperation, Ingalsbe added, "More serious legal questions are raised by your not canvassing that box."

Skaggs refused to back down and told the court, "This puts me in the position of disagreeing with our district attorney, and I certainly do." The legal minds in the room were in agreement — Box 19 should be counted and Skaggs was violating his duty, or worse, exploiting the issue to alter the outcome of the election. Skaggs would not allow the advice from the district attorney's office to trump his own personal moral code. He knew that excluding Box 19 would alter the results and Abilene would remain dry, just as he and his fellow Drys wished.

Commissioner McMillon made a motion that the court canvass all the boxes, and Felton Saverance seconded. They both voted in favor. Chapman and McDuff voted "no." As the tiebreaker, Skaggs sided with Chapman and McDuff. The motion failed 3-2. Next, Commissioner McDuff made a motion to canvass all boxes except Box 19, and Bert Chapman seconded. Now visibly frustrated, Ingalsbe sternly reacted, "You've already disregarded my advice, but I suggest that you don't do that." Another tie was broken by Skaggs and the motion passed — they would not count Box 19.

Earlier, the newspaper reported that the votes cast in Box 19 favored Abilene going wet, 511 to 354. By not counting those 865 votes, the outcome of the June 17 election was reversed. Rather than the Wets winning by 131 votes, now, thanks to Skaggs, McDuff and Chapman, the Drys — Hallelujah! — could celebrate a thirty-five vote victory. Three avowed teetotalers had just kept Abilene dry.

Those in attendance — most of whom favored alcohol sales and were there to see it come to pass — were left speechless by what obviously appeared to be a blatant maneuver to manipulate the election. Update '78 attorney Whitten was livid. Ingalsbe was dumbfounded and shocked that his advice had been ignored by a majority of the court. After all the maneuvering and head-shaking, the commissioners dismissed the morning session without formally declaring the results to be official.

When the court reconvened after lunch, Pat Dunigan, chairman of Update '78, requested that the matter of Box 19 be reopened, arguing, "When you're talking about the possibility of disenfranchising more than 800 voters, it is worthy of your time and consideration." He asked Skaggs to poll the four commissioners to determine if they would like to hear more evidence for why the box should be included. McMillon and Saverance said, "Sure." Chapman and McDuff said "No thanks." Skaggs sided with McDuff and Chapman.

An exasperated Ingalsbe advised the commissioners that they were required by law to declare the results of their canvassing as official; otherwise the Texas Alcohol and Beverage Commission (TABC) could not accept or deny applications from anyone seeking a sales permit.

It was widely understood that for Skaggs, McDuff and Chapman, the whole matter of Wet vs Dry was a moral issue. They saw themselves as the last bastion for protecting Abilene from the sin of alcohol. A sense of morality and religious conviction led them to rearrange the chess pieces in order to keep Abilene dry. It did not seem to offend their sense of morality that their method for overturning the election was not on the legal up and up.

Before the afternoon session ended, the court made the results of the June 17 election official. By omitting 865 crucial ballots from Box 19, and by a vote of 3-2, Abilene remained officially dry, just as it had been for seventy-five years.

The crowd walked out into the stifling afternoon heat, astonished at what just happened. Indeed, they witnessed history, just not in the way they anticipated.

TUESDAY, JULY 11

The temperature topped out at 101 degrees.

A newspaper reporter asked Skaggs when he had first become aware of the boundary problem involving Precinct 19. He replied, "Well, let me think. I think someone mentioned it to me last week." Skaggs also proclaimed there had been no closed door meeting between himself and commissioners McDuff and Chapman prior to their actions the day before. He did admit he had met with both men separately but would not say what was discussed.

Whitten amended his writ of mandamus motion, specifically requesting the 42nd District Court to include Box 19 in canvassing the votes from the election.

Local second-hand bookstore owner Ben Ezzell filed a complaint with the Abilene office of the FBI alleging that Skaggs had violated the Civil Rights Act of 1883 by denying voters in Precinct 19 the right to vote. Ezzell was not one of the disenfranchised voters; rather, he made the complaint as a matter of conscience. The FBI forwarded the matter to the Justice Department.

WEDNESDAY, JULY 12

The heat wave continued. Abilene was dry in more ways than one. For the year, only six inches of rain had fallen.

Letters to the editor were published on four different pages in the Abilene Reporter-News. The nicer ones expressed dismay while others were vehemently questioning the sanity of Skaggs, McDuff and Chapman. Dr. Wayne Ramsey Jr. warned of a larger issue. "A public outcry should arise against these men who have substituted personal prejudices in the place of law. I would challenge every person who considers themselves a free man or woman to closely judge the actions of these elected individuals, not in regard to wet or dry, but in regard to the freedom of man as exhibited by the Constitution of the United States."

Update '78 backer Mel Richards took up the same argument, "The question is now far beyond the issue of wet or dry. It is now a question of whether the town is run by the people, or by special groups who will apparently take whatever measures are convenient to dictate their desires." He concluded, "The action of this governmental body is destroying the reputation of Abilene through exposure in national media, and none of it is good publicity."

Indeed, on Wednesday, a four-man film crew from NBC News arrived in Abilene to document the dust-up over demon rum. They visited the courthouse to film the controversial Precinct 19 ballot box, then went to Impact to give the viewer some necessary background. They filmed at Pioneer Drive Baptist Church to show an example of an Abilene church and then headed downtown to interview patrons at the Sound Barrier, a private club on Walnut Street. They interviewed Ben Ezzell, who in addition to lodging a charge that Skaggs violated voters' civil rights, was now actively seeking to oust Skaggs from office.

In the afternoon, Attorney Whitten subpoenaed Judge Skaggs and the county clerk to appear at Friday's mandamus hearing and compelled them to bring "all documents relating to or affecting the local option liquor election held in Justice Precinct 1 on June 17."

THURSDAY, JULY 13

The temperature reached 102.

Twenty-two voters residing in Precinct 19 filed a federal lawsuit against the commissioners court and against Skaggs, McDuff and Chapman individually, alleging they had violated the constitutional rights of Precinct 19 voters by refusing to count their votes. They also alleged that the defendants violated the Texas Open Meetings Act in breach of their oath of office. The suit requested federal judge Leo Brewster to provide a permanent injunction prohibiting the defendants from disenfranchising the Precinct 19 voters. The group also asked for $25,000 to cover attorney fees. When told of the lawsuit, District Attorney Ingalsbe made his position clear, "It is my job to represent the commissioners court, but I am under no obligation to represent them individually."

The commissioners met in an emergency session to consider hiring former district attorney Ed Paynter to assist Ingalsbe in the hearing scheduled for the following day. Paynter declared he would only assist the court if his hiring was unanimous. Commissioners Saverance and McMillon said they would not vote to hire Paynter since Ingalsbe had not requested any assistance. The motion was tabled. NBC

News was there to film it all.

In the courthouse parking lot a pickup truck bore a sign offering free tar and feathers.

FRIDAY, JULY 14

Heat and hostility soared. The thermometer was relentless, topping out at a steamy 103.

Judge Don Lane entered his 42nd District courtroom at 10 a.m. The courtroom had forty-eight seats for spectators, but a crowd of at least eighty squeezed in while more than a hundred stood outside in the hallway. The board of the West Texas Fair canceled its scheduled meeting to attend the hearing.

Whitten, arguing on behalf of Update '78, called just one witness to the stand, County Judge Roy Skaggs. When asked about Box 19, Skaggs told Whitten he did not know the election outcome would be affected by leaving out those votes. Judge Lane admonished the spectators who burst out in laughter at Skaggs' answer. "We're not going to have that," Lane told the crowd.

The hearing was over before lunch. Lane ruled that the commissioners must immediately reconvene and canvass all votes cast in the June 17 local option liquor election, including votes cast in Precinct 19. The ruling removed the "dry" certification which was the result of Monday's partial canvass. Lane's edict received a standing ovation. CBC attorney Buck Wood announced, "There definitely will be an appeal."

At noon, national news commentator Paul Harvey told his vast audience about Abilene's war with whiskey.

Later that evening, a newspaper reporter phoned Roy Skaggs at home for a comment. A recorded voice let the caller know that the number was now unlisted.

SATURDAY, JULY 15

At 6 p.m. the mercury had risen to an unbearable 109. Power outages were reported throughout Abilene as air-conditioners overloaded transformers.

The level of tension was palpable. Sniping, griping and aggravation was the pervasive mood. The *Abilene Reporter-News* editorial, in response to Lane's ruling, was titled, "Applause! Cheers! Now Into the Appeals Breech." The newspaper admonished both sides for inciting the other. However, the same writer noted that the commissioners court majority's vote on Monday was "wrong — bullheadedly wrong."

SUNDAY, JULY 16

For the sixteenth straight day the temperature soared. The high reached 105.

One small group tried to cool things down. The pastors of three downtown churches sensed that they should act. As the congregants of St. Paul Methodist, First Baptist Church and First Christian Church found their pews — along with the respective radio audiences — all heard their pastors read identical statements urging their fellow citizens to put the past week behind them. The triumvirate of FBC's Dr. James Flamming, St. Paul's Dr. Ira Williams and First Christian's Reverend Chris Diebel laid out a five-point plan to heal the city. (The pastor of First Central Presbyterian, Dr. Roger Sidener, was to be included but was on vacation.) First, they requested all votes be canvassed. Secondly, they beseeched county commissioners to not appeal District Judge Don Lane's decision to count all boxes. Third, they called on the CBC to also avoid the temptation to appeal. Next, they asked for Update '78 to be sensitive to future zoning laws when it came to the possible locations of alcohol sales. Finally, the pastors urged the city council to appoint a blue-ribbon committee, composed of members from both sides, to propose zoning ordinances.

Following morning services at First Baptist, Dr. Flamming called two of his deacons, County Judge Roy Skaggs and Commissioner Bert Chapman, to let them know of the proposed plan and to see how they were holding up.

MONDAY, JULY 17

The third hottest day in Abilene's history was recorded, three degrees shy of the all-time record of 113 set in August 2024. West Texas Utilities recorded a daily peak power usage record after the temperature stayed above 100 for nine hours.

Next to the front page story detailing the pastors' plan, the *Abilene Reporter-News* ran an editorial applauding the plea for reconciliation and praising the statesmanship exhibited by the clergy. In the spirit of cooperation, Ben

Ezzell even contemplated dropping his federal complaint against Skaggs. (In the end, he was not in an altogether charitable mood and opted to press ahead.)

TUESDAY, JULY 18

The heat bore down at 103 degrees. There was no end in sight.

The four county commissioners met in executive session with District Attorney Ingalsbe. When they emerged, Skaggs asked if any commissioner wished to make a motion to appeal Judge Lane's ruling. Chapman, McDuff, McMillon and Saverance remained silent. Then commissioner McMillon said, "I'll make a motion that we obey the order to canvass the votes." Saverance offered the second and all four voted in favor. With no need to break a tie, Skaggs had no voice in the matter. The commissioners agreed to meet two days later to carry out Lane's ruling and canvass all of the boxes, including Box 19.

That evening, one member of the CBC Steering Committee told a reporter, "I do think it is time to bind up our differences and get along with the art of living together peacefully."

WEDNESDAY, JULY 19

The oppressive nineteen-day heat wave became the third longest in Abilene history. The high was 102.

The *Abilene Reporter-News* printed the shortest editorial in the nearly one hundred years of the newspaper. It was titled, "No Liquor Vote Appeal By Commissioners Court." The full editorial read: "Good. Now if the CBC will exercise equal wisdom . . ."

Taking a cue from the pastors, the three college presidents jointly issued a statement asking for calm and reconciliation. ACU's Dr. John Stevens, Dr. Thomas Kim of McMurry and HSU's Dr. Jesse Fletcher noted, "The local option election and its subsequent complications have inflamed the passions of our citizens." The trio pledged to cooperate with orderly plans to move forward and to unify the city.

The Texas Alcohol and Beverage Commission reported it had given out twenty-six applications for various types of liquor permits in Precinct One. It advised all applicants that the approval process could not begin until the election was recanvassed and, after that, it would still take three to four weeks before any licenses were issued.

In the afternoon, the CBC officially announced that, like the commissioners, it had decided to not appeal the ruling of Judge Lane and was prepared to accept the outcome set for the next day.

THURSDAY, JULY 20

Hot. Again.

Way back on June 7, 1902, Taylor county residents voted to prohibit alcohol sales, although an injunction kept saloons open until April 10, 1903. Now, after seventy-five years, three months and ten days, Abilene was on the verge of once more having public saloons. Unless someone else threw a monkey wrench into the works.

At 10:15 a.m., with a crowd of around fifty watching, the commissioners court convened and quickly passed a motion setting aside the July 10 canvass results which had excluded Box 19. Next, Skaggs tabulated the results from that box. To make a point, he handed the results to commissioners McMillon and Saverance, and McMillon read the tally: 511 for legalizing alcohol sales and 354 opposed, a margin of 157 and enough to give the Wets a victory.

In all, the June 17 election recorded 11,582 votes in favor of alcohol sales and 11,460 opposed. By 122 votes, the measure had passed, a margin of half of one percent. (An earlier report set the difference at 131, but a discrepancy between the tally sheets and the voter signature rosters caused nine votes to be dropped off.)

Skaggs introduced the motion to declare the election results as official. It passed unanimously. By 10:30 the meeting was over. Abilene was wet. The crowd trudged out into the Abilene heat.

By 2:30 p.m. two district supervisors for the TABC picked up copies of the order declaring the election results as official. With the order in hand, TABC could begin processing the growing backlog of fifty-one liquor license applications.

The election result applied only to Justice Precinct 1, which included nearly 100 percent of Abilene along with Hamby, Wylie, Potosi and Caps. (That part of Abilene located in Jones County remained dry.) The small town of Tye, also located in Precinct 1, would remain dry. Tye became a dry island in a wet precinct because Tye voters had twice rejected liquor in the 1960s, and the state attorney general's office advised that the outcome of a subsequent election in a larger political subdivision did not apply to a smaller, wholly contained subdivision, if voters had already expressed their wishes at the polls — and that is just what Tye voters had done. Their alcohol-free wishes remained in effect.

Two days later, on Saturday, the high temperature was only 94, ending a twenty-day run of triple-digit highs. On Sunday, it finally rained.

The process for a store or restaurant to obtain a license to sell beer and wine involved three steps: a hearing before the county judge, publication of a legal notice and, finally, approval by the TABC. At such hearings, County Judge Skaggs had the authority to deny an application if he felt approval would be "detrimental to the health, welfare or sense of decency in the community." (No hearing was required for a mixed beverage license.) The first hearing to sell beer and wine was held less than a week after the results were made official when Persie Cowley, owner of the Circle C Grocery located on Highway 36, stood before Skaggs. He approved the application in less than five minutes. Next up were two applications from the Skinny's convenience store chain seeking licenses for locations at 2718 North 1st Street (now a DK store) and a second location at 875 East Highway 80 (now the party room for Sharon's BBQ).

Following each hearing, applicants were required to post legal notices in the newspaper to advise the public and give anyone who wished to oppose the issuance of a license a fair chance to do so. Even those seeking a mixed-beverage license had to post notice. By Saturday, newspaper notices for mixed-beverage permits appeared from three restaurants — Saddle and Sirloin, The Outpost and Dos Amigos — along with two bars — the Ponderosa dance hall and the downtown club, the Sound Barrier.

The final step in the process was for the TABC to review the application and grant final approval or denial. The end of the long and bumpy road to selling alcohol in Abilene seemed very near. When the Circle C owner asked the TABC supervisor how long it would take to process his application and get the license, he was told that it should arrive in the mail in about a week. Six days later, a monkey wrench was thrown into the works. All applications to sell alcohol in Abilene were put on hold.

Despite the CBC opting to not pursue an appeal of Judge Lane's ruling, the group's attorney, Buck Wood, stood ready to represent any affected voter who wished to mount a challenge. Abilene physician Dr. Irby Fox and businessman Ron Strader wished to do just that. They filed suit, but not in Abilene's 42nd District court, rather in Austin's 200th District Court. On behalf of Irby and Strader, Wood pushed for an injunction against the TABC forcing them to halt the processing of liquor license applications. Wood argued that the earlier ruling by Taylor County's 42nd District Court

Judge Don Lane, in which he instructed the commissioners court to canvass all election boxes, could not supersede the earlier canvass in which Box 19 was excluded. And, on July 28, Judge Charles Matthews of the 200th District Court — two hundred miles away from Abilene — agreed, ruling that Judge Lane had, in fact, erred in ordering a second canvassing. Matthew's action put a stop to the issuance of licenses by the TABC. Abilene was back to being dry.

Two hours after Matthews' ruling brought licensing to a screeching halt, the TABC and Update '78 appealed directly to the state Supreme Court. The high court initially refused to hear the petition to set aside Matthew's ruling, but then the state attorney general stepped in to argue that the Austin judge had no standing in the case and that no district court had the power to override another district court. That plea, coupled with a further re-urging by the TABC, served to change the court's mind. The Texas Supreme Court set September 20, nearly two months out, as the date to hear the case.

Circle C, Skinny's, the Sound Barrier and some fifty-odd other Abilene establishments would just have to wait a bit longer to find out if they could, in fact, sell alcohol in Abilene. The whiskey war drug on.

The Texas Supreme Court justices heard the case right on schedule. At the end of the ninety-minute hearing on the morning of September 20, the high court quickly and unanimously ruled that the Austin judge had no standing in the matter and, in a rare move, the court took the unusual

move of announcing its ruling immediately. By 11 a.m., the
TABC district supervisor in Abilene was no longer bound by
a ruling from the Austin judge. After that, things happened
fast.

Before Wood or any other attorney could throw up a
roadblock, the TABC issued beer permits to Circle C and
the two Skinny's locations. By 1:30 p.m. a truck from Terk
Distributing, a wholesaler based at Impact, began unloading
beer at Skinny's Convenience Store No. 5 on North 1st Street.
Skinny's management sent over four additional employees
to help handle the crowd as the parking lot quickly filled.
The man stocking the shelves from the rear of the case was
simply handing the beer to hands poking through from the
other side.

From Stamford, the Coors beer distributor, Bill Reed,
delivered 750 cases to the two Skinny's stores that afternoon
and 2,000 more cases on day two. In forty-eight hours, an
estimated 45,000 cans of beer had been sold in Abilene —
one beer for every two Abilenians.

A six-pack of Coors sold for $1.75, the same was priced at
$1.99 at Pinkie's in Impact. Skinny's undercut Impact prices
for Schlitz, Miller, Budweiser, Pearl, Lone Star, Colt 45, Old
Milwaukee, Michelob and Lowenbrau. Some eager beer
buyers popped the top and enjoyed an amber brew in the
Skinny's parking lot, a violation that could have resulted in
the TABC closing the store. But the TABC district supervisor
felt it best to look the other way. It had been a long hard fight
for Abilene.

One local teetotaler, who had never bought alcohol in her life, sensed the historical significance of the moment and went out and bought herself a six-pack which she took home and set on a shelf as a conversation piece. The Abilene police reported there was only one alcohol-related arrest on September 20; it occurred at a private club.

The day after beer began flying off the shelves of convenience stores, the Sound Barrier, at 389 Walnut Street, began offering mixed drinks. Earlier that day, club owner Mark Beebe had flown to Austin in order to pick up the club's license and was back in Abilene by mid-afternoon. At 4:30 he made the first purchase in the formerly private club. The Sound Barrier was now open to the public, and bartenders no longer needed to ask to see a membership card.

Despite the rising flow of alcohol in stores, clubs and restaurants all across Abilene, the dry forces made one final attempt to alter the liquor vote, filing an election contest suit contending the initial canvass, without Box 19, was the valid count. In December, the case was heard in the 42nd District Court with Judge Lane stepping aside so that visiting Judge Dick Starley could hear the matter. Starley's thirteen-page handwritten opinion arrived in the district clerk's mail on January 2, 1979. Starley ruled against the Drys, declaring that the inclusion of Box 19 was valid and that more votes were cast in favor of the local option proposition than were cast against it. Abilene was legally wet, so long as no one appealed the ruling.

On February 13, 1979, attorney Buck Wood informed

reporters that he would not file any more appeals on behalf of the dry forces. For the first time in 241 days, there was no pending courthouse action contesting the June 17, 1978, local option election. The eight-month legal battle between Abilene Wets and Drys had come to an end. The whiskey war was over. It would take a bit longer for the bitterness, resentfulness and animosity to subside.

In one of several "on-the-street" interviews conducted by a newspaper reporter, Lila Binkley, an employee at the Merle Norman Cosmetics Studio in River Oaks Shopping Center, seemed to capture the mood of many, "I just want them to shut up about it. I don't care whether it goes wet or dry. Abilene's been the wettest dry town around anyhow." CBC treasurer, and staunch dry proponent Neil Fry said, "I'd like to see another election. Best two of three. We've won one and they've won one." Few, if any, had the intestinal fortitude to take up his proposal.

By the end of 1978, the TABC reported there were 103 locations in Abilene with some type of alcohol sales permit.

Traffic at Impact quickly fell to a trickle. Four weeks after beer was available in once-dry Abilene, Dallas Perkins announced the closing of his Impact Liquor Store, noting, "Our traffic has dwindled down to absolutely nothing." His near monopoly as an alcohol oasis came to end after sixteen years. A week later, Pinkie's Impact store began a stock reduction sale and soon relocated to the smaller Impact Food Mart location. In November 1979, Pinkie's applied for a permit to sell alcohol in Abilene at 5050 South 14th Street, opening for business on December 14. Perhaps out of sheer stubbornness, Pinkie Roden kept the Impact store open for a while longer.

Epilogue

Seven months prior to the June 1978 local option election, Roy Skaggs announced he did not plan to seek re-election once his term expired on the last day of 1978, a date marking the end of his sixteen years as county judge. He had no idea that, before then, there would be a local option election that would turn his final months, and his world, upside down. In his last five months as county judge, Skaggs held eighty-eight hearings for liquor applications. His last official act occurred eight days before he stepped down when he approved four more applications to sell beer. On what would have been his last commissioners meeting, held on December 29, 1978, Roy Skaggs opted out, taking a vacation day instead. The new county judge was James McMillon, the nephew of Precinct 4 commissioner Jake McMillon.

Precinct 1 Commissioner Bert Chapman was also not in attendance. He was in the hospital recuperating from two heart attacks. He chose to not run for re-election in 1980.

Commissioner Joe McDuff was re-elected in November 1978, overcoming a challenge by Lloyd Glick, who was motivated to run after McDuff voted to throw out Box 19. Following his loss, Glick opened a liquor store. McDuff served his four-year term and stepped down in 1982.

After thirty-six years as a county commissioner, Jake McMillon opted to not run. His seat was taken by CBC proponent Neil Fry. Commissioner Felton Saverance lost his Precinct 3 seat by fifty-seven votes in 1980.

Despite a checkered past, Pinkie Roden managed to reshape his reputation in his later years. In 1979 he received the Liberty Bell award from the Ector County Bar Association and in 1984 was recognized for his business accomplishments by Texas Commerce Bank with its Silver Bar award. He had already been named the Outstanding Citizen of Odessa by the Odessa Chamber of Commerce and was subsequently elected to the Odessa Business Hall of Fame. A historic plaque in Odessa commemorates the life and business empire of Tom "Pinkie" Roden. In January 1987 Pinkie sold his chain of twenty-six liquor stores to his brother. At the time, Pinkie's Inc. was among the top ten largest retailers of alcohol in the country.

At the age of seventy-seven, Pinkie Roden died of cancer on February 27, 1989. He was buried in a private service at his Madera Springs Ranch in the Davis Mountains. The original Pinkie's Liquor Store in Abilene is still in operation on South 14th Street.

Impact remains one of the smallest incorporated communities in Texas. The fight to create Impact ranked as the number one news story in the *Abilene Reporter-News* for 1960, 1961 and 1962. The case of Perkins v. Ingalsbe is taught in many Texas law school classes.

Following the death of Nancy Perkins at age seventy-eight in 2004, Dallas Perkins sold their Impact acreage, including their home, the city hall and the former liquor stores.

Dallas Perkins passed away in Abilene on September 22, 2017, at the age of ninety-two. In accordance with his wishes, there was no funeral or memorial service. He was buried beside his wife in the city cemetery. The only mention of his passing in the Abilene newspaper was a letter to the editor written by James Bertrand, his former neighbor at the Mesa Springs Retirement Center, who described his friend as a financial genius.

By chance — or, maybe as an answer to prayer — in 2013, the former Pinkie's liquor store in Impact became home to a church.

Grape Street billboard directing traffic to Impact.

Impact Votes
Wet, 18 to 2

September 19, 1961

Unloading boxes of liquor at Pinkie's liquor store in Impact on December 21, 1962. The store opened the next morning.
Courtesy Abilene Reporter-News.

*The scene outside Pinkie's on opening day. December 22, 1962.
Courtesy Abilene Reporter-News.*

*April 17, 1963 headline announcing the end of the struggle to
incorporate Impact, Texas.*

December 22, 1962. Dallas Perkins, center, buys the first legal bottle of whiskey sold in Taylor County since 1903. Left, John McCown, manager of C.C.H. Liquor store, right, Impact attorney Dan Sorrells.
Courtesy Abilene Reporter-News.

Pinkie's package liquor store on Impact Drive, circa 1965.

Dallas Perkins, mayor of Impact, Texas, his wife,
Nancy, and their children Oliver, Lora Lee and
Dallas Jr., in 1965.
Courtesy AP

Impact Home of Dallas and Nancy Perkins in 1978.
Courtesy Abilene Reporter-News

Dallas Perkins, 1978
Courtesy Abilene Reporter-News

June 18, 1978 headline announcing results of the local option
election that approved liquor sales in Precinct 1 of Taylor County.

Taylor County Judge Roy Skaggs handing Box 19 election results
to commissioner Felton Saverance, July 20, 1978.

Front page of the Abilene newspaper on September 21, 1978, showing brisk business at Skinny's on North 1st.

In 2024, Impact Drive is blocked by a gate.

PART TWO:
Other Hometown Commotions

The Seat of Taylor County

In 1864 Texas governor Richard Hubbard approved the selection of Buffalo Gap as the temporary county seat of the newly created Taylor County. It was not a difficult choice — Buffalo Gap was the only town in the county. Then, in July 1878, the temporary title was formalized: Buffalo Gap was the county seat.

As the Texas and Pacific Railway put down its tracks on its westward march across Texas in 1881, it sought the path of least resistance. In the business of railroad building, flat landscapes always trump picturesque hills. Track locators surveying Taylor County in late 1880 opted to cross the flat northern part of the county, avoiding the Callahan Divide that was the setting for Buffalo Gap.

The T&P auctioned off lots for the new railroad town of Abilene in March 1881, and many in Buffalo Gap saw the handwriting on the wall: soon, even with its less interesting landscape, Abilene was set to eclipse Buffalo Gap in importance.

By the fall of 1883 the growing population of Abilene had far outpaced the economic opportunities afforded in the tiny county seat. So, with a brashness that many in Buffalo Gap found cheeky, Abilene pushed for a county election to move the seat from the Gap to burgeoning Abilene.

Taylor countians braved the rain and slush to make their wishes known on October 23, 1883. The outcome surprised no one. By a 3 to 1 margin, voters chose Abilene. (For Abilene - 905, for Buffalo Gap - 269.) The *Dallas Weekly Herald* carried a report from Taylor County in which the writer noted, "The county seat here will be of advantage to Abilene, and the Chief of the Western Prairies will continue to grow and prosper." For many in the Gap, it sounded like gloating.

The Buffalo Gap newspaper, *Live Oak*, made a dire prediction about what might happen when officials from Abilene attempted to move the county records: "The attempt would not only be a willful, flagrant, knowing, open violation of law, but would be the cause of reckless and useless shedding of human blood, and the taking of human life, and the plunging of two communities into scenes of sadness and woe." In the end, there was no actual plunging into sadness nor woe and the records were peacefully brought north to the new county seat, where Abilene was already taking bids for construction of a courthouse.

Buffalo Gap resented the loss of the county seat and that resentment began to fester. So, after stewing about it for thirty years, Gappers pushed for a do-over. And, in 1913, they got it. A group in the Gap — calling themselves the Justice Club

Buffalo Gap Wants County Seat Moved From Abilene

Town Organizes "Justice Club" to Avenge Action of Thirty Years Ago—Petitions Circulated.

Abilene headline announcing the 1913 effort to move the county seat back to Buffalo Gap.

and whose membership happened to include everyone in Buffalo Gap — petitioned for a new election, claiming the 1883 election was rigged. And to raise the stakes, the county had just passed a bond to build another new courthouse; so the 1913 election would not only again decide the county seat but also where the new courthouse would be built.

The Justice Club distributed flyers countywide urging a return of the county seat to its rightful home and accusing Abilene of stealing it by fraudulent means. The Club noted that Buffalo Gap was in the middle of the county, not stuck up in some corner like Abilene. Further, the Gap had better water and scenery. And it now had its own railroad since the Santa Fe line came through.

The *Abilene Reporter* ran near-daily editorials pushing for Abilene to remain as the county seat. The newspaper took issue with a central argument put forth by Buffalo Gap — that it was located in the center of the county — pointing out that, in fact, it was four and a half miles east of the geographical center. The campaign committee pushing to keep Abilene as the county seat turned to scripture to make its case. "He who will not provide for his own is worse than an infidel. (1 Timothy 5:8) Will you be an infidel to Abilene on May 10th?"

In a front page editorial, Abilene's esteemed Judge Kade Legett wrote that the charge by Buffalo Gap that the 1883 election had been stolen and needed to be avenged was "an unparalleled outrage." He added, "It is unjust, unmerited, uncalled for and untrue. It is an assault upon the honor, character, integrity and honesty of a struggling pioneer citizenship, many of whom have done more for their country, for God, for humanity, than some of those assassins of character could do in a 1,000 years." In the same issue, the editor noted that Buffalo Gap had a host of drawbacks, such as no paved streets, no waterworks, no sewerage, no electric lights and no gas.

Like the 1883 election, the 1913 vote was not close either. By more than 2 to 1, Taylor countians voted for Abilene. In Abilene there were only twenty-four votes for Buffalo Gap. The one election box from Buffalo Gap contained 120 ballots. In it were 119 votes for the Gap and one from a confused person who voted for Abilene. (And was no longer welcome at the Justice Club meetings.) Following the Abilene victory, a poem by Milo Shackelford appeared in the newspaper:

The votes have all been counted, the battle has been won,
The old men joined the army,
and brought with them their son.
We would have thought the Gap unworthy,
if she hadn't made a fight,
But we had to have the court house —
we already had the site.

You Buffalo Gap folks must forget that we ever fought,
For we have from the very first
given this our earnest thought.
We have learned our lesson well and our teacher
we all love,
And to the Gap we are sending
a sprig by that wonderful dove.

Our hearts go out to our old-time friends
we have known for years,
We had to do just what we did,
though it brought them many tears.
Now let's all of us get together and end our little strife —
We can admire our new court house the balance of our life.

Sunday Movies and the Paramount Theatre

Simultaneous with building his Abilene hotel, Horace Wooten also constructed the adjoining Paramount Theatre in 1930. He then leased the theatre to Publix Corporation of New York who opened the Paramount on May 19, 1930. (In case you're grading me on spelling, for some reason the Paramount has always used the British spelling of 'theatre.' So, I am following its lead and writing this like a proper English lad.) The Paramount was a local marvel. By the thousands, Abilenians flocked to the Spanish-themed theatre with never-before-experienced touches such as moving clouds, a starlit ceiling and, most notably, air-conditioning! For opening night, the Paramount debuted with a world premiere showing of *Safety in Numbers*, described as "a gay romance of modern youth" and starring Buddy Rogers. An estimated crowd of 3,000 came downtown for multiple showings and to experience the chilled air.

Publix sent out one of its top men to manage the theatre. Twenty-nine-year-old Al Fourmet left the Texas Theater in San Antonio to come to Abilene and guide the destiny of the Paramount. Within weeks of its opening, he had guided it straight into a buzzsaw.

Barely two months after opening, Fourmet announced that he would make an obvious adjustment to the theatre schedule: the Paramount would show movies on Sunday afternoons — just like most every other theatre in America. At the Tuesday announcement, Fourmet naively remarked, "Imagine a city this size without a Sunday show!" In fact, the citizens of Abilene had imagined that very thing back in 1921, when city commissioners banned such unholy activities. To make that earlier ordinance official, it was signed by the mayor at the time, Dallas Scarborough, and the city attorney, Ben Cox.

In deciding to open the Paramount on Sabbath afternoons, the young manager had unwittingly crossed the Rubicon. He had also crossed a sizable segment of the Abilene population.

The day after his announcement, the three college presidents — Drs. Sandefer, Hunt and Baxter of Simmons, McMurry and Abilene Christian — condemned the move and called on local pastors to make their voices heard. Such a desecration of the Sabbath could not stand. Aptly, the first Sunday movie was titled, *Grumpy*, which precisely captured the feelings of the presidents and pastors.

The day after the announcement, a delegation of clergy

visited with mayor Thomas Hayden and the city attorney seeking assurance from the elected officials that they planned to enforce the 1921 Abilene city ordinance outlawing such activity and prodding them to seek the maximum $50 penalty should a movie be shown. Separately, the ministers huddled together and planned a sanctified barrage of sermons addressing the topic on Sunday.

The Thursday edition of the newspaper carried a Paramount ad touting "Sunday shows will be inaugurated this coming Sunday." First Baptist Church took out an ad titled "Sunday Movies" to inform the public that pastor Millard Jenkens would preach on that very topic at the Sunday night service. The ad promised, "He is going to take off the lid. We start at 8 o'clock and there will be anything but a dull time at the Old First Church"

The Abilene board of city commissioners met on Friday and passed an ordinance forbidding any movie house from showing a movie on Sunday without a license. If the ordinance was violated, a theatre risked forfeiting "their right of continuance to do business in our city." And, just to add teeth to the thing, added, "any person who violated the provision was to be deemed guilty of a misdemeanor and face a fine between $10 and $200 for each offense." The ordinance would take effect after a second reading and public notice, not in time for Sunday.

On Saturday, county attorney Frank Smith conferenced at the courthouse with city and county law enforcement representatives to make their plan should Paramount manager Fourmet actually spin a movie reel on Sunday afternoon. "This a war to the finish," Smith told a reporter.

Anticipating trouble, Publix secured the services of two Abilene attorneys should they need to get Fourmet out of the clink. The two attorneys were none other than the duo who had signed the 1921 blue law forbidding Sunday movies — former mayor Dallas Scarborough and former city attorney Ben Cox.

As expected, Fourmet opened the Paramount doors on Sunday. By 1:15 p.m. a small crowd began to gather by the door, including city patrolman Ed Cornelius. At 1:45, the box office opened and a twelve-year-old boy handed over two dimes, purchasing the first ticket to Abilene's first Sunday show. Someone in the crowd remarked, "And a little child shall lead them." As others handed over their coins, they told box office attendant Minnie Loflin, "This should help pay the fine."

At 2:00 p.m. the lights dimmed and *Grumpy* was cast upon the Paramount screen. Twelve minutes later, five officers, including Abilene police chief Ruck Sibley, walked in and arrested Fourmet in the theatre lobby. They did not actually haul him to jail; in anticipation, Fourmet's attorney arranged for a pre-signed $100 bond. The guarantor was theatre owner Horace Wooten. The officers left a few minutes later assured that Fourmet would be in county court on Monday to face charges.

The back-to-back showings of *Grumpy* provided a record day for the Paramount. Receipts were triple the amount of a regular weekday, and attendance for Abilene's first ever Sunday show was huge as thousands succumbed to temptation — and a chance to wile away a couple hours of a hot August afternoon inside the air-conditioned theatre — with attendance topping out at 3,381, exceeding the crowd for the grand opening in May.

At the end of the Sunday night service at First Baptist, the congregation unanimously passed a resolution commending county attorney Smith and local law enforcement for their actions earlier in the day.

On the following Wednesday, Fourmet's trial took place. It was moved to the city auditorium at Fair Park to accommodate a crowd of more than 350. Seated in the front row for the two-hour trial were the ministers of First Baptist, First Methodist and Central Presbyterian. Following a mere five minutes of deliberation, the six-man jury handed Fourmet the maximum penalty of $50. Juror J.H. Beasley admitted he had attended *Grumpy*.

Dallas Scarborough announced that his client would be offering another movie the following Sunday.

For the second Sunday, Fourmet showed *The Silent Enemy*, an epic tale filmed in the wilds of Canada. Again, a large crowd arrived, hoping to see the movie but also interested in the fate of Al Fourmet. Once again, right on time, he was charged with violating the law. Officers then went upstairs to arrest projectionist Leon Hansard.

The week proved to be a busy one for Fourmet. On Tuesday he was in court appealing his conviction from the week before. On Wednesday he answered charges of violating the city's 1921 blue law. On Thursday, he had to face censor charges related to *Grumpy*. On Friday, Hansard was tried, but a hung jury was unable to reach a verdict. On Saturday, Fourmet was back to face censor charges for *The Silent Enemy*.

For the third Sunday movie, the Paramount presented *Free and Easy*, a comedy — rather like the one that took place in the lobby, as this time Fourmet, along with three members of the staff, were arrested: Hansard for a second go around, and cashier Minnie Loflin and doorman Dan Castles were tossed into the mix.

By the end of the week, the scorecard for all charges read: three convictions, three acquittals and five cases pending.

Prior to the fourth Sunday show, Fourmet received a telegram from the Dallas office of Publix advising him he had been relieved as manager of the Paramount. He refused to step down and five days later was reinstated, just in time to announce that the show for Sunday would be the farcical comedy, *Let's Go Native*, starring Jack Oakie and Jeanette MacDonald. The usual arrests took place.

On Sunday number five, Fourmet showed *Holiday*. He and the rest of the Paramount staff were arrested at the usual time. For Sunday number six, it was *Song o' My Heart*, but with a twist in the role of law enforcement. Per tradition, everyone was arrested for violating the 1921 ordinance and all posted bond on the spot, but now the recently passed ordinance requiring a city-issued permit to operate on

Executive from Paramount Publix in the projection booth on opening day May 19, 1930. Manager Al Fourmet, back row, second from left.

Sunday was in effect. The ordinance additionally provided that any theatre operating without a Sunday license would also lose its license to operate on any weekday. So, manager Fourmet, projectionist Hansard, and doorman Martin were arrested and actually taken to the nearby police station to be booked on a charge of operating the theatre the past Monday. Ticket booth operator Minnie Loflin was not arrested on the new charges since she did not work weekdays. While the Paramount crew was at the police station, the first reel of Song o' My Heart was completed, so by the time Hansard got back to the theatre, the audience had been patiently waiting for eight minutes. Thirty minutes after loading the second reel, the police arrested all three men once more, this time for operating the previous Tuesday. Again, hauling the trio off to the station, again, the reel finished, again a lull — this time for twelve minutes — while all waited for Hansard to hustle back to the booth. He got the next reel loaded only to be arrested a third time, for operating the prior Wednesday; but before leaving this time, Hansard showed Minnie Loflin how to change the reel so there were no more interruptions. Fourmet, Hansard and Martin were subsequently re-arrested for crimes committed on Thursday and Friday as well.

On Sunday number seven, it was *The Sea God* and a repeat of the constabulary nonsense from the previous week.

For Sunday number eight, *Dough Boys*, a Buster Keaton film set during World War I was shown. Police were preparing a new tactic, this one involving chains and padlocks. The plan was to lock the Paramount doors just as the theatre opened at 2 p.m. But, around 11 a.m., attorneys Scarborough and Cox got wind of the plan. They quickly filed a petition in the 104th District Court. By noon, the petition was delivered to Judge W.R. Chapman at his home, and he issued an injunction stopping the police from chaining the doors, thus allowing several hundred Abilenians to enjoy the antics of Keaton.

On the Friday before the ninth Sunday show, Publix and its manager Al Fourmet threw in the towel. The city won. Publix agreed there would be no more movies shown on Sunday. In return, all pending prosecutions against the Paramount staff were dropped and the city rescinded its standing order to padlock the theatre's doors on the Sabbath. Publix issued a statement through San Antonio attorney J.J. Strickland stating that Publix "had been misinformed about the desire of the majority of Abilene citizens for Sunday shows." Strickland noted, "After two months of such operation it is evident that we were misinformed. Let's forget this small controversy and go on with our civic development." In November, Al Fourmet was transferred to Daytona Beach to manage the Publix theatres in that city.

A year later, in October of 1931, three of the four city commissioners voted to adopt an ordinance permitting Sunday movies. In a rare move, the new mayor, Lee York, vetoed the action of the commissioners; in an even rarer move, the city commissioners overrode the mayor's veto. And by November 8, Sunday movies were back on the big screen as the new Paramount manager showed *Alexander Hamilton*.

However, the three pro-movie commissioners indicated they were willing to bow to a public referendum on the matter if such was requested and, if the public sentiment leaned anti-movie, they would rescind the ordinance. The Ministerial Association quickly made the request for a referendum. Although not legally binding, commissioners committed to respect the public's wishes. Movie proponents pointed out that Abilene, like the rest of the country in 1932, was going through an economic depression that, frankly, was depressing, and movies were a needed distraction from the widespread financial woes. The college presidents, along with

ministers and a sizable crowd from each of their flocks, took
the opposite view. They ran ads admonishing, "Remember
the Sabbath Day and to keep it Holy." On Sunday, prior
to the Tuesday election, the Paramount showed *Heartbreak*,
which pretty much summed up how the losing side would
feel in forty-eight hours.

The vote took place on Tuesday, January 12, 1932, and
the heartbreak was keenly felt by those who favored Sunday
movies. The movement to legalize such activity went down
in defeat, 1004 against to 779 in favor. (One factor might
have been that, in January, folks had forgotten about the
beauty of air-conditioning on a hot summer Sunday.) City
commissioners ended the short-lived renaissance of Sunday
cinemas.

Five months later, on June 4, 1932, without any warning
Publix closed the Paramount Theatre indefinitely — along
with theatres in twenty other Texas cities. The company never
offered a definitive reason for the move, simply claiming low
revenue forced the closure. But many in Abilene jumped to
the conclusion that the lack of Sunday ticket sales brought an
end to the Paramount. However, in July the Paramount, and
fourteen other theatres, were sold to W. E. Paschall of Dallas,
a former executive with Publix. He planned to reopen all as
soon as possible.

A second citizen referendum occurred in August. This
one was proposed by a group of city business leaders and
spurred on by the owner of the Paramount building, Horace
Wooten. The group felt the closing of the Paramount offered

a real chance for angry voters to push for Sunday movies. So, for the second time in less than a year, voters returned to the polls on Saturday, August 20, and this time the movie-starved public approved Sunday shows. Four days later, the Paramount reopened, featuring the Marx Brothers in *Horse Feathers*. Once again, Abilenians could enjoy both a Hollywood film and air-conditioning on a Sunday afternoon. However, it was agreed that no movies would end later than 7 p.m. After all, you needed to leave movie-goers time to get to evening church services.

Abraham Lincoln Junior High School

Abilene High School assistant principal James "Bob" Nail, age forty-eight, was tapped to be the first principal at a new Abilene junior high known unofficially as Central when it opened in the fall of 1955. Nail's new job literally came to him, because the new junior high would open in the same building in which he already worked, the soon-to-be vacated Abilene High on South 1st Street. The high school was moving to a brand new campus on North 6th.

In preparation for his new assignment, during the spring of 1955, Nail visited with the students who would be attending the new school in September to get their input on a school name along with their thoughts on school colors and a mascot.

At the regular school board meeting on May 9, 1955, Nail reported to trustees that students named black and white as their preferred colors and they wanted their mascot to be a longhorn. Additionally, they had overwhelmingly voted for the new school to be named in honor of President Abraham Lincoln. The school board unanimously approved all of the students' choices.

Two days later an editorial in the Abilene newspaper applauded the students' choice of Lincoln, and cursory research claimed it was the first school in Texas to honor the past president. (In fact, at the time, at least four other Texas cities had Lincoln elementary schools.) Editor Frank Grimes noted that he was the son and grandson of a Confederate soldier and the nephew of several others, but he commended the Abilene students for choosing to remember "a great American."

There was a swift response to the editorial and to the school board's endorsement of the Civil War president. After the editorial ran, the newspaper printed a letter to the editor from Jewel Scarborough, who wrote to "protest vigorously against the naming of the new junior high for Abraham Lincoln," and pointedly took exception to the opinion that Lincoln was a great American. She added: "The students who made the selection of Lincoln, because of their age, and the fact that they have not yet had many history courses, would hardly have selected Lincoln to honor and to emulate, unless the teaching in their history classes had influenced their thinking, and taught them to discredit their own brave, patriotic ancestors."

Mrs. Scarborough's husband, and the former mayor of Abilene, Dallas Scarborough, soon followed up with his own lengthy letter. While he was mayor, the school building that was soon to be known as Lincoln Junior High was constructed and the bronze plaque next to the front door listed his name. In his letter, Scarborough wrote, "I am going to ask the City Commission for permission to go up and chisel my name off that building if it is going to be named Lincoln. I want no part of it."

Others wrote to commend the students' selection of Lincoln and to urge that some in Abilene quit fighting the Civil War. Max Polen wrote to reprimand Mrs. Scarborough for her assessment of Lincoln, and he included a chisel so that Mr. Scarborough could indeed get his name off the school plaque.

Also jumping on the anti-Lincoln bandwagon was the local chapter of the United Daughters of the Confederacy, who unanimously voted to protest the naming of the new school after Lincoln. Four Daughters of the Confederacy wrote to the newspaper editor to "plead with the honorable board of trustees to disregard the suggestion of immature junior high school students as to the selection of Abraham Lincoln as a name for the new junior high school, a building so dear to us all." Two of the Daughters had taught in the building while it was Abilene High — English teacher Bobbie Clack and history teacher Mamie Barnes. In their letter, the ladies went on to suggest more appropriate honorees, such as Albert Sidney Johnston, John Reagan, Stonewall Jackson and General Robert E. Lee.

In 1957 trustees of the Abilene schools named a new northside elementary for Johnston, and in 1959 a new school on Hartford Steet was named for Confederate Postmaster General John Reagan. A new school on North Pioneer was named for Lee in 1960, and in 1961, after considering sixteen other names, the school board opted to name the newest southside school for Stonewall Jackson. An editorial in the newspaper read, "It is hard to imagine any Abilenian would find fault with the board's choice." (In January 2021, Jackson was renamed to honor Dr. Joe Alcorta, Johnston became Eugene Purcell Elementary, Lee was changed to honor Robert and Sammye Stafford, and Reagan took on the name of its street address, Hartford. Alcorta, Purcell and Stafford were all local educators.)

Two months after the school board accepted the suggestion of the students to name their new school for Lincoln in May 1955, the hubbub had died down. The board never considered another name for the new junior high. On Tuesday, September 6, 1955, a total of 921 students showed up as the first to attend Abraham Lincoln Junior High.

Editorial Discord

Abilene had three daily newspapers in 1885. Two of them did not get along. Namely, the *Abilene Reporter* and the *Magnetic Quill*. They were at odds over free range vs barbed wire, and the editors regularly sniped at each other in print. Tension was on the rise. The editor of the *Reporter* was thirty-year-old Charles Gilbert. The editor of the *Quill* was thirty-three-year-old William Gibbs.

Following a trip to Alabama to visit relatives, Gilbert returned to Abilene on April 21 only to read more blather spouted about him in the *Quill*. Gilbert was hotter than a pistol. And so he went and got his pistol — along with his horse whip — and set out to find Gibbs. Gilbert and his brother-in-law, Abb Wilson, then headed to the offices of the *Quill*. Gibbs was not around, so Gilbert went ahead and laid into the typesetter, Taylor Thompson, with his horsewhip, inflicting several cuts. Then Gilbert and Wilson went looking for Gibbs. The two newspaper men met up around 5 p.m. in front of the bank on the corner of North 2nd and Pine Street.

Gibbs informed Gilbert and Wilson that he was headed

home to comfort his wife, who had learned of the attack on Thompson, but that he would return and give Gilbert all the fight he wanted. But Gilbert was in no mood to wait around. Without a word, he struck Gibbs on the arm with a heavy blow from the butt of his whip. Then both men quickly drew their pistols. In all, five shots rang out, with one grazing the brow of Gilbert. The other four sailed wide of either editor. A state ranger named Gillespie, who happened to be in town, rushed over to put a stop to the nonsense and arrested them both.

The third Abilene newspaper — the *Taylor County News* — took great delight in reporting the affair. As did other papers across the state. Headlines included, "Two Fool-Fighting Editors," "Pious Editors on the War Path," "Editors on the Shoot: A Serious Pistol Affray in the Streets of Abilene" and "A Lively Fracas Between Two Fire-Eating Newspaper Men."

Gilbert was tried for attacking the typesetter. He was fined $200, while his brother-in-law was acquitted. Gilbert appealed, was retried and fined $150.

Shortly after the 1885 Pine Street gunplay, Gilbert moved to Dallas to become editor of the *Daily Herald*. Gibbs sold the *Magnetic Quill* but remained in Abilene to become a preacher.

A Hanging in Abilene

On a Friday afternoon in the fall of 1891, there was a commotion on the lawn of the Taylor County courthouse. A crowd, estimated at 1,500, assembled to witness the first hanging in Abilene as twenty-seven-year-old William Henry Frizzell encountered the hangman's noose. It was Friday, November 20, 1891. (Thankfully, it turned out to be the only execution to ever happen in the city.)

The crime resulting in Frizzell's punishment did not occur in Abilene, or even in Taylor County. Frizzell murdered his wife of eleven months, Annie Brown, in Comanche but a change of venue brought the trial to Abilene. His attorneys put forth a defense of insanity; however, the jury was not buying it, and he was found guilty in March 1891 and sentenced to death. He had eight months left to live.

At the September opening of the fall term of the 42nd district, Judge T.H. Conner had Frizzell brought into court and explained that the state Supreme Court had affirmed the lower court's decision and that he was to fix the date of execution. Judge Conner asked Frizzell if he had anything to say. He replied that he had a great deal to say. "I want to make a full statement. My lawyers refused to let me take the stand and make a statement. I wanted to tell all about it, but the lawyers just set me down like a mummy and would not let me say a word." He went on to say that he had occasional spells in which he was not himself. The judge asked if that was all Frizzell had to say. "No, it ain't. I can get several witnesses." When the judge asked him to name some, he indicated he could think of several from Granbury but could not recall their names at the moment. Conner set the execution date for November 20.

While awaiting his doom, Frizzell seemed little fazed by his fate and was described as the most jovial prisoner in the jail. He amused himself by drawing vulgar pictures and fining visitors for not bringing cigars. A steady stream of Abilene citizens arrived, imploring him to repent. Fizzell happily spoke to newspaper reporters and kept conversation up as long as they would stay and listen. He even agreed to sit for a drawing that would appear in the newspaper.

One reporter called on Frizzell the day before his execution to ask if it was true he had sold his body to local undertakers. He said: "No sir, they can't pile money enough in this house to get it. I have agreed that Flint & Knapp (an Abilene undertaker) could have my remains to embalm; they agreed to furnish a metallic coffin and to send my body to my father. "

"Is it true that you have asked that the band be present to play a certain piece of music?"

"Yes sir."

"May I ask what that piece was?"

"Yes sir, Dixie."

"Has the band consented to play for you?"

"Dr. Wingo said he would let me know this evening whether they could or not."

Dr. James Wingo, pastor of First Baptist Church, served as Frizzell's spiritual advisor. He joined Frizzell on the morning of his execution as the condemned ate a hearty breakfast of broiled chicken, broiled bass, oysters and potatoes. Wingo remained with Frizzell as he later had a light lunch. Reporters called for a final interview, and Frizzell said he had been kindly treated by the jailers and that he would quit this life with malice toward no man.

Frizzell had earlier petitioned the governor for a thirty-day reprieve to have time to finish an autobiography he had in the works. The governor replied that such books did more harm than good and denied the request.

Following the late arrival of Dr. Sion Rogers — who had been out on a house call — Sheriff Cunningham unlocked Frizzell's cell at 2:20 p.m. and the three of them walked out of the jail and through the Abilene crowd assembled before the scaffold. According to the newspaper's report, Frizzell was dressed in a suit of black clothes and "Frizzell's step was firm, and, with the exception of an occasional twitching of the muscles of his face, he showed no sign of fear. At his request, Sheriff Cunningham permitted him to walk up to the scaffold unaided and without the hands of any of the officers resting on him." Frizzell took a seat atop the scaffold and Sheriff Cunningham told the crowd, "Ladies and gentlemen, it becomes my painful duty to execute one of my fellow men." He then read the death warrant.

Next, Dr. Wingo invited all present to join in a short religious service. He was assisted by Rev. Stuart, rector of the Episcopal church. During the service, Frizzell sat looking over the crowd and smoking a cigar. At the close of the service, Frizzell said: "Well people, I haven't much to say." He then went on to speak for forty-five minutes, offering advice for the boys in the crowd and encouraging them to lead a Christian life. He pointed out, "It was reported I would commit suicide, and as I was satisfied it was a sin, I would not commit it. I want to show what I had in my pocket for over nine months." And reaching in his pocket, he pulled out a small four-bladed pocketknife, which he said was a present from his wife and that he wanted to die with it in his pocket. Sheriff Cunningham agreed the request should be granted.

After thanking the officers for their uniform kindness, he announced he was ready at 3:15. The sheriff adjusted the ropes, tied Frizzell's arms and legs, and placed the black cap over his head. At this juncture, Frizzell asked the crowd to sing a hymn and Rev. Wingo led in "What a Friend We Have in Jesus." He then requested to hear "Never a Day So Sunny." Once the chorus died down, Frizzell turned to Sheriff Cunningham, "That's all. Good-bye to all." Cunningham sprung the trap at 3:21. At 3:36, County Physician Dr. M. B.

Crawford and Dr. Rogers pronounced Frizzell dead, and the body was cut down and put in a coffin.

The Abilene commotion was over and the crowd dispersed. Nine days later, on Sunday, November 29, 1891, Reverend Wingo made good on a promise he made to Frizzell: his sermon was titled "Lessons Learned from the Life of William Henry Frizzell."

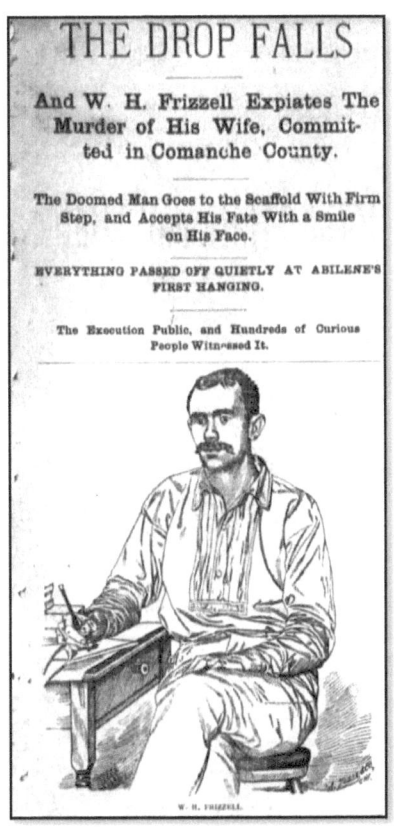

Front page of the Abilene Reporter, November 20, 1891.

Dancing

Over a five month period in late 1950 and early 1951, the Abilene High School gym on Peach Street became the epicenter of one of the most contentious debates in Abilene history. It began one day in early December 1950 when a group of Abilene High students approached principal Charles Romine to ask if the school would sponsor a dance in the Eagle gym. Mr. Romine instantly concluded that such a decision was above his pay grade. He knew that no dance had ever taken place in the gym or, for that matter, in any Abilene school building. Or, for that matter, within eyesight of any Abilene school. Romine quickly passed the request to superintendent Nat Williams, who recognized a hot potato when handed one. He wisely sent it up the chain of command.

And that is how seven innocent school board members looked down one day and found that a moral hand grenade had landed in their laps. At a school board meeting one week before Christmas 1950, that grenade exploded. The resulting shockwave rocked the very foundations of several Abilene churches.

The board meeting was packed. Three Abilene ministers representing First Baptist, University Baptist and St. Paul Methodist, their cups running over with ill humor, jointly offered up a thick slice of piety. They began with, "Word has come to us that certain groups of the school have requested the use of the high school gymnasium for the purpose of social dances, i.e., dances in which men and women dance in arm and arm embrace." There were audible gasps. Pastor Sullivan of First Baptist told the board that participating in social dances "paralyzes one's spiritual powers." It was unclear what that meant. The ministers then pointed out "that teachers and pupils who were conscientious objectors to dancing would be embarrassed by the school system's sanctioning dances."

Next, the clergy presented a three-page petition opposing the use of taxpayer-provided facilities for such an abomination, listing several reasons for taking a stand against the depravity. For one, it was pointed out that, "When young people hold each other in a close embrace while bouncing around the dance floor to torrid music, they cannot help but be sexually stimulated if they are physically normal."

Following lengthy and highly charged public comment — and often involving scripture — bravely, school board member R.B. Leach, who was a Presbyterian — at least for a few minutes longer — made a motion to permit dances in the yet untarnished gymnasium. Mr. Fraley, whose name was listed on the rolls of St Paul Methodist, offered the second, but his voice caught. The vote to allow dances on school

TRUSTEES SPLIT, 5-2

School - Sponsored Dances Okayed; Ministers Object

Abilene Reporter-News announcing the school board's decision to allow school sponsored dances on December 18, 1950.

property was then called for. Suddenly, Abilene, Texas stood on the very edge of the abyss.

The motion was approved 5 to 2. Properly supervised social dancing was authorized, and the use of school facilities for such dances could take place at the discretion of the principal. The five pro-dancers were unprepared for what was coming. For them, the walls of Jericho would soon come tumbling down. Whereas, the two who voted against dancing, Roy Skaggs and Mrs. Tom Roberts, were put up for sainthood.

Both the Old and New Testament were invoked. Pastors devoted their sermons to the subject. "There is no question to the fact that dancing leads directly to lasciviousness, drunkenness, fornication and adultery, all of which are condemned by the above passages." (See Galatians Chapter 5.) The school board members were strongly urged to repent and to turn from their wicked ways and reconsider. They stood fast, refusing to budge.

Seats on the school board were suddenly in play, with anti-dance candidates quickly filing for the upcoming election. Letters to the editor were coming in so thick and fast that, three months after the board decision, the newspaper announced it would no longer print letters on the matter. It was time to move on.

And, within weeks, there was much arm in arm embracing amongst the now-sexually awakened students inside the Abilene High School gym. Seventeen-year-old AHS senior Earl Leeson told a reporter: "All that stuff about sex stimulation would never have occurred to us if the grownups hadn't brought it up."

No Left Turns

In 1948 there was a dust-up between the city and merchants with stores on Chestnut Street.

Drivers on South 1st Street were often stuck behind cars waiting to turn left onto Chestnut, causing congestion at the intersection. Police Chief Royal Kelley and City Manager Boyd McDaniel made a study of the situation. They concluded that in order to remedy the problem, "No Left Turn" signs would be put up on South 1st. Store owners on Chestnut found there was an immediate and sharp drop-off in business.

More than ninety merchants signed a petition claiming they were being singled out and asking why the police chief was only picking on Chestnut and leaving Sycamore and Elm wide open for left turns? The petition demanded the signs be removed or the business owners would move to secede from the city. Some merchants expressly felt that the south side of town was being discriminated against by the city, and there was strong talk of resurrecting the former South

Side Business Men's Club to lobby for the Chestnut Street businesses. Clyde Fulwiler, owner of Fulwiler Printing, said, "The businessmen over here are paying taxes just like everybody else. We're not going to stand for this new regulation." One customer who managed to reach Jack's Men and Boys' Store said he had to drive seven blocks out of his way to finally reach the store.

Earnest Nichols, manager of Piggly Wiggly in the 200 block, insisted that the merchants have a chance to meet with city commissioners to stop the nonsense. Mayor Roscoe Blankenship called a special session of the commission to receive the petition and discuss the matter.

Two days later, city manager McDaniel issued an executive order that the signs be taken down, but he pointed out, "We feel that when so many property owners and taxpayers oppose a regulation affecting their area we should grant their wishes, even when we are convinced they are wrong."

Piano Nabbing

Another bugaboo landed on city manager Boyd McDaniel's desk in 1947. This one was between the city and the once all-powerful Parks Board. In those days, the Parks Board was virtually autonomous, wielding an authority that can only be dreamed of by the current parks board. All things "parks" were its domain. And that included the municipal auditorium at Fair Park. That building went up in 1927 but by 1947 had been judged to be unsafe due to some cracks in the walls. Yet, tucked away in the auditorium was a grand piano. And the YMCA had asked to borrow it. The Parks Board denied the request.

The YMCA appealed, and the city commissioners took up the matter. The commissioners voted unanimously for the city to overrule the Parks Board and go ahead and turn the piano over to the YMCA. The Parks Board quickly protested, claiming that it alone retained jurisdiction over the piano.

It was up to city manager McDaniel to figure things out. He and the city engineer went to the auditorium with a gob of keys — none of which fit any door. They then cut the lock on the stage door and helped move the piano onto a truck and delivered it to the YMCA.

The Parks Board members quickly met in an emergency session. They fired off a letter to the mayor, commissioners and McDaniel stating that, in their opinion, city officials had violated both the city charter and the constitution of Texas by handing over a city owned — albeit unused — piano to a private organization.

A 1962 change in the city charter abolished the carte blanche authority enjoyed by the Parks and Recreation Board. It became an advisory board.

The City Auditorium at Fair Park.

ÓVER PARKS CHIEF'S PROTESTS

City Manager Moves Piano, Auditorium Lock Broken

November 8, 1947.

East Abilene

The 1954 development of property around Lytle Lake set off a testy dispute, with the dust stirred up for six years.

The Sayles Company developed the acreage around Lytle, which was adjacent to the Abilene city limits but not in the city. Rumblings soon began at City Hall about annexing the property, with the lake homeowners firmly opposed to the idea.

To counter the annexation talk, lake residents decided to incorporate as their own town. In what has to be one of the most uninspired names of all time, it was to be called "East Abilene." The election to incorporate East Abilene was set for December 29, 1956.

The startled mayor of west Abilene, C.E. Gatlin, along with city commissioners, convened high level peace talks with the breakaway neighbors. The two sides agreed that if the East Abilenians would cancel the vote to become a new city, then Abilene city officials would not even bring up the word annexation again before January 1, 1960. So the election to create East Abilene was called off and the crisis was averted.

However, a few months later, Abilene voters elected new folks to lead the city. Jesse "T-Bone" Winters replaced Gatlin as mayor, and three of the four commissioners were swapped out.

The new civic braintrust did not feel bound to the peace plan put in place by the previous administration, so they abandoned the armistice and voted to immediately annex the Lytle Lake area into Abilene. East Abilenians were livid and quickly filed suit. And lost. So they appealed. And won. The court in Eastland voided the annexation, ruling that the agreement to postpone any such talks until 1960 was valid. So the city commissioners undid the annexation and set East Abilene free. Of course, such judicial matters take time. And only a few months after de-annexing, the calendar turned to 1960. Seven days into the new year Abilene re-annexed Lytle Shores.

Homes in "East Abilene".

Fishing at Lake Abilene

This commotion pitted local fishing enthusiasts against a variety of forces who felt public safety far outweighed the right of any Abilene angler.

Abilene constructed its first lake in 1922, neatly tucked in the hills above Buffalo Gap, and it was only a matter of time before folk began clamoring to cast a lure into the muddy waters of Lake Abilene. With a straight face, it was dubbed "The Gulf of West Texas." If Lake Abilene were a fish, you'd toss it back for being too small.

Water from the lake arrived in Abilene (thanks to gravity as no pump was necessary) and the citizens quickly took to watering their yards and gardens. Flowers began to bloom in abundance, a welcome anomaly in arid West Texas.

The lake was Abilene's first municipally-owned reservoir. Lytle Lake was older but was the property of West Texas Utilities and not widely open to the fishing public. In April 1924 Judge Demarcus Oldham requested that the city allow fishing on the waters of Lake Abilene and suggested that an annual permit cost $10. Further, he presented a list of 230 local fishermen willing to fork over the money to cast their lines into Lake Abilene. Former mayor E.N. Kirby protested; he was not opposed to fishing, he was opposed to the $10. He pushed for citizens to be allowed to fish at no cost, "I love to fish — and I catch them too — and can pay for a permit, but I want to see Lake Abilene used by everybody who can avail themselves without cost." He did caution that he thought all fishermen should cast their lines from the bank, not from a boat. He advised the commissioners, "Restrict them to fish from the bank. Nearly every one of these men who have signed up to take permits, chews tobacco and spits promiscuously, and I know it." No one wanted city drinking water contaminated by those spitting fishermen. They vowed to not spit. Along with the list of fishermen willing to pay for the privilege, Oldham presented a statement signed by twenty-one Abilene doctors asserting that there was no risk to the public.

The commissioners listened to Oldham and acted. On the first reading, three of the four commissioners voted in favor of the fishing ordinance, while commissioner Oliver Hale and mayor Charles Coombes opposed the idea. But before the second and final reading could be presented, the floodgates opened. In a newspaper editorial, Mayor Coombes came out strongly against fishing, citing public safety as his reason. The Texas State Health Officer, Dr. Malone Duggan, concurred and pointed out that a typhoid epidemic once

Lake Abilene in the 1920s.

took hold in another city after a camper pitched his tent next to the water supply. The *Abilene Daily Reporter* took up the matter, writing in opposition. The editor pointed out that risking the health of the people of Abilene trumped the momentary pleasure of fishing. The paper agreed with the mayor, "The Mayor is right, you can't regulate the number of times a tubercular spits on his bait and throws it into the water which we drink. Why take such chances?"

Within days of the commissioners vote to initially approve fishing, six of the doctors who signed the earlier statement rescinded their approval saying they had signed it without giving the subject serious thought. Dr. Ray Maddox, a dentist, had put his name to the initial statement, but when asked by a reporter if he still felt it presented no public health concern, Maddox said, "I do not. At first consideration, and because I am a fisherman, I thought so. But now I do not think it should be permitted." Another earlier signer, Dr. Stewart Cooper, reversed course as well, "There is no necessity for fishing at Lake Abilene and I do not believe it should be done. It would create too much of a hazard to public health." Another backslider, Dr. Wade Hedrick, was quoted by the newspaper, "I signed the petition, but I did so without any thought."

Joining in the anti-fishing chorus were the ladies of the Women's Forum. At their weekly meeting they held an hour-long discussion on the topic; they agreed there should be no fishing and the water should not be chlorinated because it would wilt their flowers. The Lions Club held a straw vote at its meeting — fifty votes against fishing and only six feeling otherwise. The vote at the Kiwanis club came in 34-11 with the anti-fishing crowd in the majority.

On the second reading of the ordinance, two of the earlier "yes" votes were out of town, so mayor Coombes and commissioner Hale outvoted the lone pro-fisherman commissioner in attendance. The new ordinance not only axed fishing but also outlawed bathing in the lake and camping nearby. Violators faced a fine between $5 and $100. The professed non-spitting fishermen would need to angle elsewhere; there would be no fishing at Lake Abilene.

Seven years later, in 1931, with four new city

commissioners and a new mayor in place, the subject of fishing on Lake Abilene was back on the table. Mayor Lee York was opposed to the idea, but the four commissioners were not fully on board. At their first meeting, the fishing debate took precedence over weightier matters, such as how to meet the city's financial obligations during the Great Depression. The newspaper admonished the new city government for spending more time discussing fishing and not near enough time tackling the budget woes. The newspaper dubbed the group the "Fishing Commission." To put the matter to rest, the newspaper suggested a referendum on the matter and even offered to foot the expense of the election.

Instead, commissioner Clover Johnson made a motion to allow fishing at Lake Abilene as well as at the recently completed Lake Kirby. It passed unanimously. Beginning on May 1, 1930, fishing permits went on sale, costing fifty cents for Lake Abilene and twenty-five cents for Kirby. The ordinance specifically prohibited spitting in either lake.

The Ambushing of Texas Tech

Bad blood boiled mightily over in March of 1936. A few Abilenians — along with several travelers who happened to be driving along that portion of the Bankhead Highway known locally as South 1st — witnessed the biggest street fight to ever take place in the city. The epicenter of the fracas was the Cities Service gasoline station at the southeast corner of Sayles Boulevard and South 1st with it spilling over into the street as well as the adjacent T&P right-of-way. For twenty minutes collegiate combatants brought traffic to a standstill with a very uncharacteristic Abilene street brawl.

At the heart of the matter was wounded pride. The tale began a year earlier in September of 1935 as the Texas Tech Matadors (prior to the Red Raider mascot change) came to town to take on the Hardin-Simmons Cowboys in a Friday evening football tilt which included some fisticuffs mixed in as Tech took a 9-0 victory. Three players were ejected in the course of the match, and the final whistle brought athletes and spectators onto the field with words exchanged and indignation starting to simmer.

The following year Tech coach Pete Cawthon turned down a proposal for a Texas Centennial game in Dallas between the two teams on the grounds that the Cowboys would not be much of a draw nor would they present sufficient competition. It was on the heels of this libel from Lubbock that the Matador band happened to come to Abilene for two days of presenting concerts.

The Tech group arrived late on Thursday, March 19, and checked into the Hilton Hotel on Pine Street. Later reports claim that all Matador band members went straight to their rooms and to bed. Yet sometime after midnight an HSU campus monument went missing. The light cannon, which had been given by the War Department following World War I as a memorial to the lost boys of Simmons, and which had faithfully guarded the campus entrance undisturbed since 1919, turned up missing. The near-sacred cannon was discovered early the next morning guarding the across-town campus of McMurry College. McMurry students pled innocent to the prank and laid blame on the visiting band boys from Texas Tech.

The Friday evening band concert drew a crowd of 500 to the Abilene High auditorium to listen to the Matador musicians. Among those in attendance were some HSU faithful who surreptitiously set off a stink-bomb just before the first note sounded. Towards the end of the concert, a rear door to the auditorium opened and three eggs splattered on stage. And still, the night was young.

Following the concert, a party of Tech bandsmen went to a downtown dance hall and there encountered an even larger group of HSU Cowboys bent on a counterblow to the cannon snatching. Ten of the Techsters were cornered, kidnapped and hauled off to an unknown lair where the scientifically-minded Baptists applied silver nitrate to the foreheads of their captors spelling out "HSU" in a temporary branding.

Prior to heading north to Lubbock the following Saturday morning, the band presented a short concert at Abilene Christian College before loading up on their two buses. Thus, the stage was set. As the Matador buses entered South 1st at Grape, the occupants were blissfully unaware of a Baptist bushwhacking lying in wait just six blocks to the west.

A horde of Hardin-Simmons students had gathered at the Cities Service station ready to defend their school's honor and have the last word as the cannon-thieving Tech boys rolled by. Armed with sacks, baskets and boxes stuffed with mostly fresh eggs, the ambuscade was set. As the first bus entered the crosshairs, the air on both sides of South 1st was filled with arcing cackle-grenades splattering and spraying in a reprisal of satisfaction.

Anticipating the buses to meekly pass through the barrage, the boys of HSU were a bit taken back when a twist in the plot occurred and the lead bus came to a screeching halt, spewing out the Tech faithful. At that point, assailants remained in a comfortable majority with the assailed accurately assessing their unbalanced chances. But soon,

HSU-TECH FEUD
* * * * * * *
ENDS IN BRAWL

Abilene Morning Reporter-News, March 22, 1936.

the second bus pulled in behind the first and the odds tilted Lubbock-ward. What had been nervous HSU laughter mixed with a fair amount of Tech shouting adjusted itself to full-on shouting from both sides. The collegiate horseplay quickly turned into group warfare followed by man-to-man combat. Bottles and sticks flew along with fists as Matadors and Cowboys each stated their case.

Passersby traveling through on South 1st joined in with a good sampling of Abilenians to take in the fracas. And, to keep the police from learning of the melee, a student guarded the gas station telephone. After fifteen minutes a general exhaustion set in with both schools falling back to tend to their wounded. Bruised bandsmen were loaded onto the buses and clobbered Cowboys were hustled into cars for a northward retreat. Cities Service attendants tried to restore some civic goodwill and washed dripping eggs from the besieged buses. By 1 p.m. the Matador Band was gladly headed out of Abilene.

The brawl was front page news, with McMurry president Dr. T.W. Brabham explaining that the school's night watchman discovered the cannon around 2:15 Friday morning and immediately went to the men's hall, only to find them all asleep. Tech band director D.O. Wiley firmly stood by his insistence that his boys had no role in the removal of the cannon, while HSU president Dr. J.D. Sandefer pledged drastic punishment and expressed his utter outrage at the rowdiness of his students.

The HSU-Tech brawl would be the number one topic of conversation in Abilene over the next few days as the feud was told and retold. Most of the smart money was bet on the "sleeping" boys of McMurry.

Mayor Lee York and Commissioner Clover Johnson

The commotion between mayor Lee York and commissioner Clover Johnson had its origins in the fishing ordinance pushed through by Johnson in 1931. York opposed fishing at Lake Abilene, but at the first meeting of the new commission Johnson ignored York's take on the matter and made a motion to allow fishing. The motion passed.

York and Johnson made it a habit to be on the opposite sides of a number of issues. Commissioner Johnson did not want the city to annex property along Sayles Boulevard east of McMurry College. York, on the other hand, very much wanted it annexed. Johnson wanted to lift the ban on the showing of Sunday movies; York favored continuing the ban. With the financial constraints brought on by the Great Depression, Johnson proposed that the mayor and commissioners take a pay cut. Again, York opposed

York Wields Waste Basket In Fuss With Johnson

Mayor Lee York.

City Commissioner Clovis Johnson.

Johnson's suggestion. York wanted to fire the city employee hired as the lake keeper for Lake Kirby. Johnson wanted to keep the man on the job.

Once, in a moment of heated public debate, York proclaimed that Johnson was a disgrace. Johnson shot right back, characterizing the mayor as a "jellyfish." All of this was leading inexorably to a climax, with their relationship dipping to its lowest point in 1933.

The final bone of contention was Johnson asking when Mayor York would give up his office following York's re-election loss. In the 1933 mayoral race, York had drawn three opponents. One of them was Commissioner Johnson. In a political ad, Johnson noted, "It is true we have had some unusual things to happen that were not so harmonious. I know I have made mistakes. I am not as much of a reprobate as some would try to make you believe." By a mere sixty-nine votes, Johnson prevailed over York.

According to the city charter, an outgoing mayor would step down at the first meeting following the election, or as soon thereafter as practicable. The next meeting was three days after the election, and it was obvious York had no plans to step down so soon. Johnson asked York about his plans, and York said he would relinquish his chair once the city audit had been completed. During this exchange, the meeting room at city hall had six people in it — the mayor, the four commissioners, and a lone reporter from the Abilene newspaper. The presence of the newsman is the only reason we have an account of what happened next.

The discussion between York and Johnson quickly rose to a full-blown argument. The reporter described what happened, "York interrupted Johnson saying, 'I've had all this I'm going to.' He stooped down, grasped the wastebasket at his left, pushed back his chair and walked to Johnson's side of the table. Not a word was exchanged as the mayor brought the wastebasket down twice on Johnson's head and arm. Commissioner Sammons jumped up, took the basket from York and passed it across the table as York returned to his seat. The encounter was a matter of seconds and the city secretary and city attorney, returning a moment later, knew nothing of the occurrence. It remained quiet for some time, the air supercharged. Somebody commented on a passing topic and all fell for the change in conversation."

Three days later, York entered a guilty plea to a charge of simple assault brought by the city attorney. He paid a fine of $7.50.

Mayor-elect Johnson was sworn in a few weeks later following completion of the audit. In what had to be a terribly awkward moment, outgoing mayor York administered the oath of office to his adversary. They did not shake hands.

Not Tonight Henry!

Following three drafts and several boisterous hearings, the first reading of a city ordinance with the stated purpose of addressing the "onslaught of obscenity, filth and trash" and "to protect the morals of our young people from the influences of obscene and lewd movies" was unanimously approved by the city commissioners on April 6, 1961.

Due to an overflow crowd, the commission met in the library auditorium. The required second and final reading of the ordinance was set for two weeks later. The ordinance would create a nine-member Citizens Review Board authorized to shelter youthful eyes and innocent minds from any objectionable movies scheduled for Abilene movie screens. (The board would also get a say on any vaudeville performances, plays, operas, floor shows and musical comedies which might occur in the city.)

According to the ordinance, ten days prior to the first showing of any movie, theater owners were required to provide the title to the board. If the board found an objectionable film headed Abilene's way, they could step in and protect the underage crowd by issuing a classification ranging from A to E. Movies rated "A" were suitable for all ages while a "B" kept out those under twelve. However, if a movie received an objectionable "C" or "D" rating, the theater would be required to post a public notification at the box office advising that those under age eighteen could not attend. Should the theater fail to post such a sign, it could incur a $200 fine. Movies receiving an "E" rating would be banned from being shown anywhere inside the Abilene city limits. Members of the Citizens Review Board played a pivotal role in Abilene society: they were to keep out the smut. Unique to American censorship laws at the time, the Abilene ordinance also provided for fines to be levied against parents should their underage child see films rated as objectionable.

At the second reading of the ordinance, the commission again met at the library in order to handle the throng of interested citizens. Joining the crowd was Bill Becker, a reporter from the New York Times, along with a film crew from CBS-TV. (Because the CBS film cartridges lasted only a limited time, everything came to a halt every eleven minutes so a new cartridge could be loaded into the camera.) Before the public comment began, Mayor Cearley Kinard told the public he would not tolerate any outbursts, jeers or heckling. For more than two hours, interested citizens passionately spoke their minds. One speaker liberally employed scripture to punctuate the need for the ordinance, while two teenagers each presented a petition — one signed by 767 students and another with more than 500 names — opposing passage of the ordinance. Abilene attorney Beverly Tarpley, representing local theater owners, spoke out against the idea, questioning its constitutionality and contending that the board would be forced, in most cases, to judge a picture without seeing it since exhibitors rarely got a film ten days in advance of showing it. Abilene Christian College President Don Morris spoke in favor of the rating system, with his remarks drawing applause from the like-minded. After listening to the prolonged debate, commissioners unanimously passed the ordinance. Tarpley pledged to appeal the commissioners' action. The Motion Picture Association vowed to fight the law as well.

Becker's *New York Times* article included, "Abilene is noted for its high winds and high concentration of churches. The brisk north winds sweeping down from the Panhandle sector keep the wide streets clean. Moral cleanliness is ministered to by more than 100 churches and three denominational schools."

The new ordinance took effect May 1, 1961, with Mayor Kinard naming four women and five men to the Citizens Review Board. They were set to meet the first Wednesday of each month to pass judgment on the upcoming slate of movies. At their first meeting, 100 movies were approved while six others had their rating withheld until the board could view the films, including *Desire in the Dust* and *Diary of a High School Bride*. (Both were later given "B" ratings.)

The first real test of the new law came in June when the

Tower Twin Drive-In, owned by Kathryn Jacobs, planned to show a film titled *Never on Sunday*, a romantic comedy about a free-spirited Italian prostitute with a mind of her own. (It was nominated for six Academy Awards, winning for Best Song.) Based on the film's storyline, the board members assigned it a temporary "C" rating until they could watch the film and make a decision based on primary knowledge.

If a scheduled movie received a rating of C or below, the theater owner had to be served notice. Assistant City Attorney Truman Kirk — accompanied by one board member, a police sergeant, and a photographer from a local television station — went to Jacobs' home to serve notice of the C classification assigned to *Never on Sunday*. After the photographer surprised Jacobs with his camera flash, she slammed the door in their faces and Kirk was unable to serve the notice.

Attorney Tarpley said that Jacobs would not deny anyone entry nor would notice of the rating be posted. Should the Citizens Review Board come to see the film, Jacobs urged them to come in just two or three cars so as to not take up too much space. On opening night, bumper-to-bumper traffic extended a quarter of a mile past the Tower Twin entrance and more than 150 cars were turned away as the parking lot filled. The eight-night run of *Never on Sunday* brought in more than 12,000 movie-goers, one of the biggest draws ever at the drive-in. Mrs. Jacobs, along with theater manager Duane Gates, were cited for failing to post signs calling attention to the film's restrictive rating.

Within days of the showing, a state law was passed that prohibited Texas municipalities from controlling the distribution of any movie bearing the seal of the Motion Picture Association. So, on the advice of the city attorney, the charges against Jacobs and Gates were dropped. The new state law rendered the Citizens Review Board moot. To counter the new legal landscape, Abilene city commissioners amended the obscenity ordinance and put the burden on theater owners. The owners would need to assign movie ratings themselves and publish the rating in any advertisements for the film. Failure to do so would result in a fine. To police the revised ordinance, the city commissioners created a new board known as the Exhibition Review Board composed of the same nine people who had comprised the defunct Citizens Review Board.

Six months after her first brush with the law, Kathryn Jacobs was in trouble once more. In addition to the Tower Twin, she also owned the Crescent Drive-In on South Treadaway where, on December 4, 1961, she showed a "near-nudie" movie titled *Not Tonight Henry!* in which Henry dreamed of "amorous escapades with sirens of the past." The Abilene police swept in. It seems that Henry's fantasies well exceeded allowable standards by some distance, resulting in confiscation of the film and the arrests of Jacobs, the Crescent manager, the projectionist, and the ticket-seller (who did not even have a clear view of Henry). All were charged with violating the ordinance provision making it illegal for anyone to "willfully exhibit or willfully assist in the exhibition of a motion picture which is obscene." Seven of the nine Citizen Review Board members had seen *Not Tonight Henry!* and unanimously agreed it was, in fact, quite obscene. Jacobs noted, "If these movies hurt the morals of Abilene people, then the board members must be awful by now."

Once again, Beverly Tarpley represented the Crescent crew. At the trial of Kathryn Jacobs, held in January 1962, the six-person jury heard prosecution witnesses describe the film as "lewd," "suggestive," and "immoral." It was characterized by one review board member as appealing "to the depraved thought and exotic desires." In order for the six-man jury to judge for themselves, they walked from the courthouse over to the Palace Theater on Chestnut to get a look-see at *Not Tonight Henry!* (The film was still in the possession of the police as trial evidence.) Police officer Shelby Fancher, who moonlighted as a projectionist at the Palace, handled the movie equipment for the special screening.

The trial, including the sixty-three-minute movie, lasted only one day. However, the jury could not reach a consensus; four were ready to convict but two others were not all that offended by Henry and his prurient interests. The hung jury resulted in a second trial six days later. For the retrial, the court once more rented the Palace Theater to show the evidence. This time the screening was open to the public and more than 100 spectators opted to join the jury to see what Henry was up to. The second trial produced a conviction and a $100 fine for Jacobs. Tarpley appealed the conviction.

When the case came before County Court-at-Law judge

Theo Ash in March, Tarpley requested that Ash dismiss the case. Aiming to prove that legislating morality is a fool's errand, Tarpley walked into court with a box of evidence. At the counsel table, she displayed a lamp she had purchased at a local store showing half naked mermaids. Next to the lamp, Tarpley arranged several magazines of dubious taste that she had picked up at an Abilene newsstand. Then she argued that the city ordinance and state statutes were in direct conflict.

Judge Ash expressed his own agreement with the establishment of local obscenity laws as well as his support of the city's efforts to protect Abilene youth, but he agreed with Tarpley: state law superseded the local ordinance. He dismissed the case against Jacobs. Charges against the manager, projectionist, and ticket-taker were later dropped and the confiscated reels of Not Tonight Henry! were returned to the Dallas distributor, who agreed to not send any other near-nudie movies to Abilene.

On November 1, 1968, the Motion Picture Association of America began voluntarily rating movies, thus relieving Abilene theater owners from that task and ending the need for an Exhibition Review Board to assure the ratings were being assigned.

The Heart Balm Trial

One surefire way to create a commotion and draw a crowd is the combination of a sensational story and no fee for admittance. And that is why the Taylor County courthouse was packed to the gills during a run of hot July days in the summer of 1931. A heart balm trial was playing out at the courthouse.

Heart balm is a term you don't hear much anymore. It refers to a jilted fiancée who files suit for breach of promise; thus, seeking a "balm" for her broken "heart." Typically, the balm being sought was in the form of cold hard cash.

The most sensational heart balm trial in Abilene involved a lovely local lass, twenty-one-year-old Madge Roberts, who brought suit against the dark-haired Louie Keel, a rancher from Roswell. Madge claimed that the breach of promise brought on by the dashing Louie caused her mental distress and loss of weight.

Madge was beautiful but not too well off financially. She worked at the cigar stand in the lobby of the Wooten Hotel. Louie, on the other hand, might best be described as rugged and rich. He also was fairly helpless in warding off his own hormonal urges. And it was that chink in his armor that drove him into the tobacco-stained clutches of Miss Madge. After Louie spotted Madge at the Wooten, he was unable to resist her pretty face and provocative form, and he quickly exhausted the arrows in his flirtatious quiver. To bolster his charm offensive, Louie even hinted at marriage— a hint Madge took at full face value. Louie's blandishments left her with the distinct impression she was, without a doubt, his only love. He, on the other hand, was more of the mindset that Madge was simply one, among many, of the females frolicking in the field in which he was playing.

So, when word first reached Madge that Louie was already married to an unsuspecting girl named Lillian, well . . . the news sent Madge straight to bed; then to the hospital where, according to her lawyer, it took four doctors to look after her and her weight dropped from a healthy 120 to a gaunt 95. Madge was diagnosed with something called "nervous intestinal contractions," a condition that her doctors felt was brought on from the romantic shock and subsequent despair. In her suit, Madge claimed she was despondent, nervous and irritable, all due to Louie and his deceptive nature.

At the trial, the courtroom proved inadequate for accommodating the crowds as people drove for miles to sit in on the real-life soap opera. During the day and a half that Madge was on the stand, the courtroom was so packed that one fellow passed out from the crush. The halls were filled, people stood in the doorways and anterooms. No one dared leave for the restroom for fear of losing their spot.

Trial testimony was daily front page news. If you read the trial proceedings you will quickly pick up on the fact that Madge was not nearly as keen on suing Louie Keel as was her gold-digging mother — who was keen to the tune of $50,000 and ownership of a house on Palm Street.

Mom even went to Campbell's Dry Goods Store and spent $23 to dress her daughter in an all white outfit and white hat. Madge showed up on day one donning her matrimonial white with a now-unwarranted bridesmaid in tow. Madge recounted her embarrassment and the physical pain of being contractually deserted. The whole affair was rife with intrigue and sexual overtones, all too sensational to miss. The crowd oohed and aahed when Pete Wiggins testified that, on a double date, he had looked in his rearview mirror and saw Louie and Madge in the rumble seat of his Ford kissing with an elevated degree of passion.

Louie's defense would go on to show that Madge was, indeed, a very good kisser and had apparently practiced her skills far and wide and not limited solely to the lips of Louie. Madge sat with her head down, tears flowing freely.

When Louie got his turn on the stand, he claimed he never promised marriage to Madge and that she was a bit too literal.

Next, both a bellboy and the switchboard operator who worked at Abilene's Hilton Hotel testified of seeing Madge getting off the elevator with her boss — not Mr. Keel — and of them snuggling and kissing. By now, the crowd was fanning and swooning and not just because it was 101 outside.

The soaring temperatures did not diminish the daily throngs who clamored for a seat. Keel's attorney, Tom Blanton, said he sweated off twelve pounds during the steamy trial. Madge's lawyer claimed he dropped five.

In all, the trial lasted eleven days with the stenographer filling 1,100 pages. Finally, the all-male jury was sent to the jury room to deliberate. When they finally emerged — and to the great excitement of the crowd — the foreman announced that they were deadlocked, 5 to 7, meaning the whole thing had to be repeated in November. And, in what looks like a ratings move — wouldn't you know it! — the retrial also came down to a deadlock, 9 to 3, with the jury tilting in Madge's favor.

The third installment of the Abilene Heart Balm Trial was to be held in the summer of 1932 but, instead, both sides agreed to abide by a two-judge arbitration panel. In the end, the judges decided in favor of the defendant. So Louie Keel was off the hook and the people of Abilene were denied a three-peat of the heartbreak drama. Louie was assessed court costs, but was immediately awarded a judgment against Madge to recover that amount, so he paid nothing.

Louie and his lawful wife Lillian went on to be married for forty-nine years, presumably happy. As for the jilted Madge Roberts, five years after the trial, she married bachelor Joe Bailey Fry.

Some states have repealed laws that once provided

recourse to soothe a broken heart. Texas has not. So don't be proposing marriage willy-nilly to every heartthrob you run into.

Myrtle

When ten billboards for Abilene Clean and Proud went up around Abilene in late summer of 1997, they received more attention than ever intended. It turned out, they were a marketing home run.

Abilene Clean and Proud was formed in 1985 as part of a nationwide effort known as Keep America Beautiful. Abilene joined with more than 370 other cities participating in the program which aimed to rid litter and trash from the streets while also beautifying the city by sprucing things up and planting flowers, bushes and trees. (In 2000, Abilene Clean and Proud changed its name to Keep Abilene Beautiful while maintaining the same purpose.)

Abilene Clean and Proud introduced Make A Difference Day to the city in 1992. The idea was for folks all over town to get out for a one day blitz and clean up their neighborhood. The local coordinator for Make A Difference Day was Janet Ardoyno who instigated and oversaw a variety of projects, from painting homes to planting 25,000 daffodils. But it was the 1997 effort that produced the greatest response. Ardoyno, along with Abilene Clean and Proud director Donna Albus, wanted to blanket Abilene in crepe myrtles. An order was placed for 5,200 crepe myrtles in varieties of reds, pinks and purples that could all be planted on Make A Difference Day. In order to promote the effort, Ardoyno had the idea to market it through a clever billboard. And that is when the commotion started.

On the right side of the billboard was a silhouetted woman wearing a long dress and a wide-brimmed hat and who apparently had been a regular at the gym based on her hourglass curves. In huge letters, alongside the Clean and Proud logo, the text read, "Myrtle's coming! Get your bed ready." A phone number was prominently displayed below the text. The idea was to pique the public's curiosity; in turn, they would call the number and wind up placing an order for some crepe myrtles to brighten up their front yard.

However, a sizable number of Abilenians interpreted the billboard message much differently. To them, the billboard was about s-e-x, pure and simple, and the coquettish and curvaceous Myrtle was offering a bit more than simply a reminder to call and reserve some bright blooming bushes. One offended Abilene lady remarked to a newspaper reporter, "The meaning that is most clearly presented is one with a sexual innuendo. There's nothing in that billboard about flowers at all." The husband of the offended woman added, "I don't think there's any doubt that it's a sexual pun." Albus was quick to point out that Myrtle was coming to town for a visit and so you should get the flower bed and/

Abilene Clean and Proud billboard that started the commotion.

or the guest bed ready. Albus incredulously asked, "Does the word 'bed' mean that you're going to do something sexual?"

Following a front page story in the *Abilene Reporter-News* that presented both interpretations of the billboard, the slanging match got underway. Letters to the editor poured in, and the local brouhaha was reported in newspapers across the country and in at least two Canadian provinces. It was front page news in Galveston and Alexandria, Louisiana, and ran on the inside pages in scores of other papers. The story of Myrtle was aired on CNN, and the October 6 issue of *Newsweek* noted the controversy.

In one letter to the editor, the writer took Ardoyno to task, "I would think Church of Christ members would be embarrassed that the person who came up with the idea of this billboard claims association with their denomination."

Others wrote to commend Ardoyno for improving the look of Abilene with her beautification efforts. Another shamed Albus for suggesting there was not a double meaning in the billboard, "Of course the billboard was intended to have sexual innuendo. That's what sells in America." But most letters called out the narrow-minded, accusing them of being a bit mimsy and over-moralistic. One writer admonished, "Get a life. Sex has been around since day one. Read your Bible, first page."

After a week of printing multiple letters each day, the *Abilene Reporter-News* ran an editorial saying "It's time to put the Myrtle issue to bed, so to speak." The paper was done printing letters on the matter.

Meanwhile, the phone at Abilene Clean and Proud was ringing off the hook. The 5,200 crepe myrtles quickly sold out and more were ordered. Make A Difference Day 1997 was a huge success. Abilenians — some prudish, most not — spent the day planting 8,369 crepe myrtles. Today, you can drive all over Abilene and see the bright pink, red and purple blooms that Myrtle caused when she climbed into our beds all those many years ago.

Acknowledgments

The memory of Dallas Perkins Jr., not only filled in many of the blanks and details when it came to sorting out the story of Impact but kindly passed along photos. Likewise, Lynn Ingalsbe provided insight into the 1978 local option liquor election. Ron Erdrich took time to help me navigate the files of the *Abilene Reporter-News* and retrieve photo negatives from sixty years ago which Steve Butman expertly turned into positives for the book.

None of this would have happened without the urging of Glenn Dromgoole. He not only had the idea of telling *Abilene's War With Whiskey* but he expertly edited the text, correcting my grammar, punctuation, and Oxford comma omissions.

About the Author

A native Abilenian, Jay Moore believes sharing local history strengthens our sense of community. His books include *Abilene Daily, Abilene History In Plain Sight, Abilene A to Z,* and *Legacy: The Dodge Jones Family and Foundation.* He co-authored *Abilene Stories* with Glenn Dromgoole and Joe Specht.